Screwing Up

How one MP survived
politics, scandal
and turning forty

Screwing Up

How one MP survived
politics, scandal
and turning forty

Mark Oaten

biteback

First published in Great Britain in 2009 by
Biteback Publishing Ltd
Heal House
375 Kennington Lane
London SE11 5QY

ISBN 978-1-84954-007-0

A CIP catalogue record for this book is available from the British Library.

Designed and typeset by SoapBox
Printed and bound in Great Britain by TJ International

Contents

*To the people who offered friendship and love
when I needed it most*

Acknowledgements

I would like to thank everyone at Biteback Publishing, including Jonathan Wadman for his editing and in particular Iain Dale, who agreed to take on the book and has provided much support and advice. Although I hate having my picture taken, I am delighted that one of my constituents, a student, Coral Robinson, agreed to let me use her photo on the front cover.

The ups and downs of my political life have involved characters too numerous to mention, but you can't do this job without a team. I would like to thank my personal staff, who have supported me through the highs and lows and for learning to read my scrawly handwriting: in Winchester Gill Kilmartin, Lyn Anderson and Julia Harkness, and at Westminster, amongst the many talented researchers, I now count Lois Thomas, Ralph Scott, Antonis Papasolomontos, Celine Tricard, Olly Kendall, Matt Grimshaw and Owen Braben as friends. Charles Kennedy and his head of office, Anna Werrin, gave me a wonderful opportunity to grow as a politician, whilst Chris Rennard, the Lib Dem chief executive, has helped through good and bad. In the early years Paddy Ashdown's support during my various elections in Winchester was invaluable, as were my wonderful agent and chair team of Ingrid Clifford and Rodney Sabine.

To sustain a political life you need friends to keep you normal. Stuart, Mick, Fizz and Martin have been close mates since school. Alison and

Screwing Up

Chris Day and Ellis were among the many who gave me safe haven and friendship when I was involved in the media storm. Belinda's four sisters and her mother made a boy from Watford welcome in Hampshire. My own father took up his marking pen one more time to this book, for which I thank him; and, of course, I couldn't have written about the early years without countless chats with my mother, to whom I owe so much.

Finally, my thanks to Milly and Alice for letting me spend too many hours in the office and to my best friend of all, Belinda.

Prologue

Over the fence

I was going to say that we lived in the kind of sleepy Hampshire village where not much goes on, but strictly speaking that wouldn't be true. Bramdean had seen a suicide, floods, affairs and a celebrity drink-driving case in the space of a few years. Today, though, was going to top that. I had just withdrawn from running for the leadership of the Liberal Democrats and felt a real sense that I was finally off the political escalator and ready to enjoy life again. Instead my world was about to come crashing down.

Saturday 21 January 2006 started as a bright sunny morning but as I opened the bedroom curtains I thought it was odd to see two cars in the village hall car park, which is right opposite our house. I had no idea what it meant, but something inside me sensed this was trouble. I dressed quickly and marched outside to find out what was up. One of the drivers tried to hide a camera and at that moment I knew something was badly wrong. The other driver, dressed in a suit and tie, stepped out of his car and, showing me his business card, said: 'I think you know why we're here.'

In fact I had no idea. I guessed it was something to do with the leadership campaign, or more stories about Charles Kennedy and his drinking. I had been close to Kennedy and knew most of the secrets the press pack were after. The suited man said: 'We have an allegation about a male escort,' and produced a photo of someone. I immediately recognised his face even though I had not seen him for over a year. Until then it simply hadn't occurred to me that this would ever come back to haunt me.

I said very little and told them I would be going inside to talk to my family. As I walked back from the village hall to face Belinda I felt quite calm, even though my life was about to explode. As the children were starting to have breakfast I took her into our utility room and as calmly as I could, told her what I'd done. I hugged her and said I was so sorry. I stepped back, not really knowing what to expect. My heart was bounding and my mind racing – everything in my whole world was dependent on what Belinda would do next. Our two daughters sat next door unaware of how their dad had just smashed up their home life. One moment expecting all the innocence of eggy bread, the next about to see their mother torn to shreds and for what, some thrill-seeking experimentation? Belinda was clearly shocked but initially very calm, even showing pity towards me. I guess our immediate instincts as parents kicked in and we both did everything we could to act normally in front of the girls.

In my foggy mind I knew we needed help and fast. Belinda phoned trusted friends who immediately rushed round and began to discuss the practical arrangements for getting Alice and Milly into a safe place and then deciding what to do with the two of us. In many ways the horror of what I had done and the impact on our marriage was put on hold as we discussed a range of options. We thought of flying out to the Caribbean as a family, but eventually agreed that putting myself and Belinda together in an isolated setting was madness. I then called Anna Werrin from Charles Kennedy's office and she in turn informed the chief whip.

In the hours that followed there were tears, shouting, friends arriving and a growing number of journalists turning up in the village hall car park. The Liberal Democrats' chief executive, Chris Rennard, began to take control of the practical side of things. I knew I would have to say something publicly and immediately wanted to resign as home affairs spokesman for the party. We drafted a statement which would be issued later in the day and then Chris offered Belinda support with any travel arrangements she needed to try and escape. At no point did I consider facing the cameras there and then. In many ways I wish I had just walked out and faced the music, resigned and apologised. Fleeing and going to ground for days only increased the press hunt for me and kept the story running longer. But I was in turmoil and in no fit state to make decisions.

By now the house was full of friends and the plan was to use their cars to block the entrance to the village hall, trapping the photographers and hacks in the car park. My exit, however, was more of a problem. It was decided I would head to the West Country and a friend agreed to drive me the 4½-hour journey to Cornwall. His car was positioned at the end of a farm track which ran past the back of our house. Friends packed a rucksack for me and I legged it down to the back of the garden, struggled to climb over the fence and dashed for the boot of the waiting car. Thankfully we were not spotted or followed as we sped away. Sadly Belinda's exit resulted in a scrum at the front of the house, but the muscle of our rugby-playing friends was more than enough to see off some of the weedy paparazzi.

The drive to Cornwall was awful and I find it hard to recall what I was thinking. I know that other public figures caught in scandal, like Jonathan Aitken, have talked of feeling suicidal. I never felt that, but sickness and depression were starting to kick in and I knew I would need help with something like Prozac and sleeping pills. I managed to track down my counsellor, who agreed to fax a prescription through to the small fishing village where we were heading.

As the countryside sped by, I started to reflect on what I'd done. In fact there is hardly a day that goes by when I don't think of those moments. The awful walk back across the road to tell Belinda, and the extraordinary hours and days that followed as I scrambled across fields, disguised myself and fled the media attention. I can even laugh at some of it now – the near-death skiing experience whilst trying to talk to Belinda, whales in the Thames, setting a restaurant table on fire and exploding televisions.

But none of that can hide the total mess I had made of my life and the hurt I threw on to my family and friends. Within hours of the story breaking emails, texts and then letters started to pour in, about 8,000 in all. Many told of similar stories. They asked why I did it and for ages so have I. Was it a mid-life crisis, burnout, a breakdown, sexual doubts, childhood issues? They all sound like excuses, but all must play their part. Then there was life in the political fast lane – dealing with terrorism, Charles Kennedy, the daily grind of the political world – screwing up my work–life balance.

In the end the harsh truth was that there was no-one else to blame. Not a male escort, not the *News of the World*, but just me. In the months and years since the scandal broke I have begun to fit together the broken pieces of my life and in doing so understand what went wrong and reflect on Westminster and being a so-called Honourable Member. It's a weird world of expenses, crazy costumes, and the Strangers Bar. I've also been able to reflect on how turning forty, hair loss and pressure of work screwed me up – so if you're expecting another self-congratulating political autobiography, forget it. Life's far from how most politicians tell it.

1

Political virgins and Volvos

The road to Westminster had started when I decided to join the SDP and stand as a local councillor in the Stanborough ward of Watford. As I turned eighteen in March 1982 I had to decide how to vote in the local elections of that year. Thatcher had yet to get into her stride. The country was divided with riots in the inner cities and a sense that she was governing for the rich and the business world that funded her party. Labour was full of conflict: nuclear disarmament, pulling out of Europe and a battle to see off the rise of Derek Hatton and his Militant colleagues. Still heavily dependent on trade union funding, the party looked stuck in the 1970s. I didn't like what I saw in the two main parties but had little idea what the Liberals stood for!

There had never been much political discussion at home and I had no idea how either of my parents voted. In the run-up to a local by-election a Liberal canvasser, a very elderly lady called Dorothy Bramwell, knocked on the door. I said that both my parents were out and I didn't know how they voted. She then uttered words that were to change my life: 'Never mind about them, what about you?' My own background, with a father whose family was from old colonial stock and a mother with roots in working-class Manchester, made me feel slightly classless, a merger between rich and poor.

My father was born in India, son of a high-ranking official in the government. His was a privileged childhood with servants and private education at Tonbridge. I've never discussed it much with him, in fact it was only on his ninetieth birthday, when I visited him to celebrate at his home in the Italian university city of Padua, that three rather random facts emerged. First of all, his parents had lost a baby in childbirth and my grandfather had climbed the hill behind their house in Calcutta and just buried the baby without any official notification. Secondly, my father won a tennis tournament aged eighteen, the prize a packet of cigarettes, and thirdly, he rowed for Oxford in the second eight.

A Quaker and pacifist, he refused military service and drove ambulances in the Second World War. I've never been religious, but if I were then I would lean to the very simple Quaker values. I once went with him to a Sunday morning meeting as a reluctant but slightly inquisitive ten-year-old. After what seemed to me an eternity of silence I blurted out: 'Dad, when's it going to start?' 'It just did,' came the response. Twenty years on, I attended my second Quaker meeting on the occasion of my father's wedding to Anna-Maria, his Italian bride. This time I again broke the silence and started the service by wishing them well.

Generally, though, I don't do religion. I am too practical to accept vast amounts of the Bible and I am too cynical not to feel that religious differences are the source of too many wars and conflicts. A few years ago at a small social event at Lambeth Palace, the Archbishop of Canterbury, Rowan Williams, asked me what my religion was. I felt embarrassed to admit my lack of faith and muttered something about my dad being a Quaker. Sensing my awkwardness, he kindly glossed over it, saying: 'Ah! Good people, those Quakers!'

These days, with my own family we occasionally go to church but a family service at the village church presents a real challenge to the Oaten household. Although the service starts relatively late at eleven o'clock, we always seem to walk in during the first hymn. On one occasion we were running very late and Milly was in one of those baby rucksacks that goes on your back. As we dashed in the vicar ushered us towards the front pew, without giving me the time to take Milly out of this enormous contraption. All I could do was sit down with her hovering, distraught at what was happening, above my head. I spent until the Lord's Prayer trying to disentangle her, screaming and kicking (her, not me, that is) whilst trying to look as if I had everything under control. At that point I decided to abandon the attempt and we beat a hasty retreat.

There is no doubt I get my practical hard-headed side from my mother. Born in Manchester, she came south at an early age when her father, a printer, relocated the family to Watford. She has battled hard and used her intelligence to succeed in business despite being refused the chance to go to university by her parents. I remember her always being dressed smartly with big company cars, a briefcase and her stories about work as she sat on the edge of my bed to say goodnight.

When she was diagnosed with cancer in 1973 my world fell apart. I can still remember the moment my dad told me about her operation, the awful smell of the hospital and the sight of drips in her arms. She beat the cancer and is, over thirty years on, fit and healthy.

We lived in a safe and secure part of Watford, with a primary school that I could walk to. Nascot Junior School was just round the corner and as I got older I was allowed to walk home – unthinkable these days for a nine-year-old. I would let myself in the house and watch *Grange Hill*, *Blue Peter* or *Magpie*. Sometimes I would walk back to my best friend Geraint's, and we would play endless competitions of Subbuteo laid out on his bedroom floor until our fingers were sore from flicking our players.

There was no shortage of money or love and my memory of those days was of long, hot summer days and happy family holidays driving to Provence in our yellow Allegro. I recall early starts, throwing up on the hovercraft and my dad endlessly announcing that hotels were *complets* as we desperately sought accommodation on the long drive through central France to our destination. Eventually we'd arrive in Arles and spend a week watching the pink flamingos in the Camargue, and the bulls running through the streets towards the Roman amphitheatre, and going on countless trips to buy lavender-scented gifts for my grandparents. The smell and sounds of Provence with its pine trees, crickets and mistral wind were to install in me a love for France which remains today. I'd love to have bought a second home in the south of France but have always been too loose with money to have saved enough. Belinda and I recently took our two girls to the region, showing them the sites of Nîmes and Avignon and taking them on a kayak trip under the Roman Pont du Gard aqueduct. It felt like a life had gone full circle, bringing the next generation to discover these delights.

My mother gave up work to look after me until I was old enough to go to school, then as both my parents worked I spent many days with Nana and Granddad. They both loved gardening and some of my fondest memories are of time spent helping out on their allotment site in Garston.

Over the years I've taken great comfort in gardening. I am at my happiest in my greenhouse with 5 Live's football commentary as my companion whilst I pot up and transplant seedlings. Maybe it's a womb-like experience but there is something reassuring about the warmth of the greenhouse as rain knocks gently against the glass. I find it reassuring that seeds are sown, germinate, get pricked out as the months move from January to planting out towards the end of May. This annual event has formed part of my life since I first had a greenhouse at the rather precocious age of twelve. Now I often dream of just disappearing to buy a French farm and spend my days engrossed in growing rather than squeezing in the garden between all the other demands at the weekends. I've no doubt this passion comes from my grandparents. I associate them with digging, allotments and the most wonderful sets of huts and potting sheds a gardener could wish for.

My grandfather Ben was very tall, bald all the time I knew him and a large, slightly clumsy giant. He would potter around the garden and his shed, sending pots flying, bashing his head and dropping things whilst my nana would sweep up behind. A small figure almost half his size, she was the counter-balance in what was a perfect relationship. As a young boy I loved the short three-mile trip from their semi-detached house in Watford to the Leavesden allotment site. The whole palaver of getting his Hillman out of the garage, the rollercoaster drive as he ignored lights and other cars, sending me sliding around seatbeltless on the leather seats as my grandmother shouted out unheeded warnings. Then there was the fiddle of unlocking the gates into the allotments followed by the inevitable drama of them swinging back and scraping the car as we shunted in. When my parents went out I would be dispatched to spend Saturday night with my grandparents. I absolutely loved it and adored them. Turning up with a small black suitcase I would settle in for the evening enjoying the treat of staying up for *Match of the Day* and a cup of my nana's Horlicks. To this day either the smell of that drink or the signature tune of *Match of the Day* brings a lump to my throat.

A few months before I stood for election in Watford my grandfather died. He lived in the Stanborough ward, where I was standing, and one afternoon during the campaign I happened to pass his road when I saw an ambulance outside his house. I rushed in to find he'd had a stroke. He never recovered and died a few weeks before polling day. I'll never forget my grandmother helping count out leaflets the day he died or on election day itself handing me his polling card asking me what she should do with it. A former Communist activist, I think he would have been proud to see me elected as his local councillor.

I never doubted the love of my parents. I was always closer to my mother and remain so to this day, speaking on the phone many times each week. My dad played his part in bringing me up and although we never kicked a football about he was always at home until he left to teach in Greece when I was about fourteen. On a visit back from Greece when I was about seventeen he just announced to me and my mother that he thought it was time to divorce. That was it. No row or discussion. We just carried on watching TV and he went off to mark some exam papers. It all seemed very sensible to me – no big drama and frankly a happier future for my parents. Actually, it came as no surprise, as the very large age gap between my parents was becoming more evident. I am sure I would have felt differently if I'd been younger and I am slightly guilty that my parents hung on until I was older.

My father was a Latin and French teacher at the local boys' grammar school. He was an old-style professional and his teaching style was suited to the 1950s and 1960s. By 1976 his theory that all pupils were keen to learn was being severely tested and he was subjected to pranks from pupils that resulted in funeral bouquets and piles of sand often turning up on our doorstep. The thought of going to his school filled me with dread, as did the option of a stuffy private education at Merchant Taylor's. That left the local comprehensive, Queens', and thank God I ended up there. I may have missed out on better grades, but for the lessons in life I will always be grateful.

They say that you remember a particular teacher. In my case it was our form tutor Bill Grimwood, who effectively took a mixed bunch of children and turned us into rounded, relaxed young adults. His liberal attitude to lunchtimes in the pub and allowing us to raid his wine cellar helped make my time in the sixth form a ball. I enjoyed Queens' and eventually ended up, according to school reports, as a popular member of the school community. There were a few tricky times; embarrassingly my voice seemed to take forever to break, creating a range of croaky squeaks between man and child. As a consequence I dreaded reading in class. Worst was doing this in French, which seemed to exacerbate the problem. Thankfully our French teacher, Mr Higgs, took the heat off me. He was endlessly teased and spent our lessons being pelleted with small bits of wet paper blown through the empty body of ballpoint pens. Attacks on teachers were rare although I remember an English teacher having a chair smashed over his head.

I struggled academically at the school, managing just five O-levels and two Es at A-level – in English and history. Even then I had to stay on an extra year to retake the history. I wasn't disappointed, though, as Caroline, my first real girlfriend, was in the year below so it meant I got to see more of her.

After I left school I worked for myself as a gardener going round in a little white van clearing up beds and – yes – sometimes ending up in the beds of my female middle-aged clients. One way or another I grew up a good deal and had some rather wild times, even finding time for some serious landscape design work in between.

After about a year I found this too lonely, even for an only child, so I decided to sign up for a teacher training degree at nearby Wall Hall College in Radlett. I knew my mother would disapprove so for a couple of weeks I pretended I had an office job. I got up all suited and smart at 8.00 a.m., drove round the block and then pulled on a jumper and jeans before continuing to college. I couldn't keep this up for long; after all it prevented me from staying in bed in the morning, which I began to realise was one of the main benefits of being a student. I confessed all and apart from a few moans about having to support me for three more years Mum took it quite well as she funded my education.

Being a teenager then a student in Watford revolved around football, pubs and the one and only nightclub, called Baileys. To me and my mates it was the coolest place on earth – by day a dirty graffiti-covered door to the side of Caters supermarket, but at night a bit of neon light and red rope brought the West End to our part of town. I was into floppy hair, white socks, T-shirts and these flimsy black plimsolls we all called Chinese slippers. It was not flamboyant enough to be new romantic but we felt cool enough as we scuttled up the stairs to the cloakroom and into the enormous bar and stage. It was full-on 80s cheesy entertainment with live acts from David Essex, Showaddywaddy, Shalimar and, best of all, Sister Sledge, who had us all up dancing on tables. I was crap at chatting up girls but still managed to get a snog most nights. When our mate Vaughan, a blunt-talking school friend originally from Doncaster, got a job at Baileys he became the local hero. Our free VIP passes got us to the Special Bar, where the music was even louder and the rum and coke more expensive.

Of course the really cool kids of the 80s were going to see the Specials or The Beat. I was not cool. I took Caroline, my Australian girlfriend, to see 'Kids from Fame Live' and bought her a Dollar record (white vinyl, I fear) – hardly the kind of thing you admit to your friends, although she seemed to like it.

Life was great and I fell into a routine with my mates. We'd cycle or walk into Watford and spend hours wandering from Woolworths to the market in search of cheap singles for 25p before heading to Wendy's to get a burger. Feisal, a fellow footy fan, and I would then head for the same table at a window opposite Radio Rentals so we could check out the half-time scores. Then it was back to mine for full-time and to play the latest purchase on my Binatone stack multi music player that had more buttons than Concorde but basically only performed two real functions – on and off! *Hill Street Blues*, Botham bowling out the Aussies, *Brookside* and Pringle jumpers formed the backdrop to my teenage years and they were without doubt the happiest days of my life.

This rather easy childhood without political parents or any bitter social experiences meant I had no inbuilt bias towards any political party. Whilst the Liberals knocking on my door got me interested it was the new political party that really motivated me. The SDP, with its more independent, less entrenched stance, had natural appeal. I also liked the politicians that made up the Gang of Four, although I never really knew Bill Rodgers, the least familiar of them. Years later I regarded it as a privilege to sit alongside Shirley Williams in parliamentary meetings. Straightforward, intelligent and like a terrier with an issue, she displayed enthusiasm and energy that I found remarkable given she must have seen and heard nearly every single argument thousands of times during her forty-year political career.

I've only met David Owen a few times. He is slightly scary and superior and looks the same at seventy as he did when he was Foreign Secretary in his forties. In early 2004 I interviewed him when I was editor of the *House Magazine* and found him in a reflectful rather than a regretful mood over his time attempting to break the mould of British politics.

The grand old man of the SDP was, of course, Roy Jenkins, for so many, including Tony Blair and Charles Kennedy, a kind of father figure and political confidant. His biography of Truman helped me with my degree in American politics. Over two decades later, his work on Gladstone and Baldwin helped me to write my own book on coalition governments. He was a wonderful writer and I treasure a small note he wrote me congratulating me on a piece of work which he described as 'beautifully written'.

Being an eighteen-year-old member of Britain's newest political party made me a perfect political virgin. Not only did I have no background or deep interest in the political system but I was joining a party where the majority of members, whatever their age, were in a similar position. Of course we learned from the defectors who joined from Labour and we grudgingly picked up tips from our soon-to-be Liberal allies. But it was its new, fresh and slightly naive character that made the SDP both vibrant and attractive.

In 1981 a party that allowed you to join by credit card, had a strong bold logo and took no funding from unions or big business was different. It was also very middle class. In Watford, if you wanted to know where the SDP meeting was held you just looked for the car park with all the Volvos. The local leading lights were mostly businessmen – impatient, wealthy and bemused by the very idea of canvass cards, constitutions and knocking people up on polling day. They and I thought there must be a better way to do things but we soon learned to adapt to the rather quirky world of local politics.

It was our joint meetings with the local Liberal Party that caused the most amusement and bemusement. Sitting in the living room of John and Mary Taylor, the rock of Liberal Watford, you could easily pick out who was from which party – suits or beards, company directors or academics – the dividing lines were clear. We just looked and sounded different in those early days. Of course we were awfully nice to each other. The SDP crowd thought the Liberals were barmy… and heaven knows what they thought of these new, rather brash, outsiders. The Taylors' cats were quick to take sides. A vicious pair of Burmese, they would scratch and pester Social Democrats at every opportunity. More than one safe council seat was handed to the Liberals in negotiations as a result of those bloody cats as we buckled early just to save our shins. But over the months and years ahead we all grew fond of each other and by the time the Liberals and the SDP merged a decade later you truly couldn't tell the difference between us any more.

Eventually these seat discussions turned to where I might stand. I picked the ward where the Liberals had polled the worst in the whole of Watford at the last local elections. Then surely I could only improve on the result. My choice was a Tory seat called Stanborough which also had a massive council estate within its boundaries. One road stuck out and filled canvassers with dread. Rushton Avenue was the main route into the estate and door knocking was an interesting insight into the social problems of the day. Whilst the electoral roll often showed a couple living at one address, the reality was different. Mrs Batchelor would tell you that her husband was away at the moment. If you ended up concluding that he was in Brixton, or Parkhurst, rather than on a business trip to Frankfurt you'd be right.

The first few months canvassing in the area were terrifying. You would be attacked by a wild pack of stray dogs, or worse still a group of eleven-year-olds, whose chants would bring you down to size:

'Mate, you the pools man?'

'Um, no.'

'Who is you then?'

'I'm canvassing.'

'You Labour?'

'No.'

'Tory wanker!'

'No, no, no.'

'What is you then?'

'SDP.'

'What's that?'

'Look, mate, shut up, is your mum in?'

It was just like being the posh kid again at my first day of secondary school. When I turned up at Queens' from my nice little middle-class primary school I was teased for ages about how I spoke. I soon learnt to drop a few letters from each word and stop talking posh. I needed all those skills again to survive the Rushton Avenue canvass. The gang of eleven-year-olds had more than words as a weapon. In one humiliating canvass session I was chased off the estate with a water pistol and a canvass card soaked from the pistol's contents rather than the rain.

I surprised everyone, myself included, by winning them over and winning the seat. By the time of my re-election four years later walking Rushton Avenue was a humbling experience. The chants were now 'You alright, Mark', 'Let's have a poster', 'Well done, mate'. House after house now had an orange poster in it and the offers of help and support were incredible. I learnt fast that there should never be no-go areas in politics. The loyalty shown to me from folk on this estate was enormous. Many joined the party, leafleted and became mates. Tim Minchin from Florence Close was typical. He was enormous, with tattoos on every square inch of flesh and a letter on each knuckle. In any normal circumstance I would have been terrified of Tim. As it was he delivered hundreds of leaflets and offered to sort anybody out if they gave me grief. I knew he had hardly a penny to his name, but he would still come along to local party fund-raising events and we were all the richer for it. There was another change in those four years. This time the youngsters that had threatened me with water pistols in 1986 now had real pistols. Canvassing in 1990 one of them asked me into his downstairs flat. 'Mark, I'm going to make sure you win. Come in, let me show you.' I broke my normal canvassing rule and wandered into his living room. As the *Coronation Street* theme screamed from the TV, in front of his whole family he pulled up a floorboard and showed me his gun. 'There you go, I'll shoot the Tories for you.' I declined, of course. I mean, how would I explain the bullets on my election expenses?

Despite looking back on these days with affection, if I am honest the one thing I have hated more than anything as a politician is the nightmare that is canvassing. Some MPs tell you they love it – hand-to-hand interaction with the voters. They're lying!

As winter turns to spring each year political activists begin knocking on doors in the run-up to the May local elections. I even associate the early spring smells and the clocks going forward with canvass sheets and doorsteps. The whole process starts rather like the Hampshire Hunt with the meeting point. When you arrive outside the village pub the local ward organiser is meant to hand out canvass cards to the team and send you off with rosettes, leaflets and encouragement. It never happens like that. Nobody is on time and when Hilary turns up in her twenty-year-old Volvo, all the canvass cards are buried under a pile of children's football boots, old crisp packets and the dog's favourite blanket. There then follows a twenty-minute muddle trying to put the roads in order and explain to canvassers how to find Blackberry Drive. A major discussion starts on who should team up with whom before a further detailed briefing on every little local issue – none of which is ever raised on the doorstep. Giles can't find his favourite rosette, David spots a mistake in the leaflet and Susan refuses to canvass any houses near the vicarage because she's in the WI with their inhabitants – it's all rather awkward. All of this helps put off the actual task of knocking on doors – but then, just as you are about to head off, you see a team of blue rosettes heading your way and discover the Tories have just canvassed the whole bloody village before you.

Not much has changed in twenty-five years of canvassing. At the end of the day, the basic requirement remains the same – to find out how people will vote. However, you observe changes in social patterns. Back in the 1980s as I ran around the estates in Watford ringing doorbells people would answer 'Oh! I thought you were the pools man'. This century in Winchester you're more likely to get 'Oh! I was expecting a Waitrose delivery'. I am not sure if this is a commentary on geography or society, but given that I've never done the pools (too complicated) or shopped at Waitrose (too expensive), I am not in a strong position to comment.

People come to the door with all sorts of expressions. I've had them answer naked, screaming at me fresh out of the bath, crying, throwing things; on one awful occasion a lady expected me to act as undertaker and remove her husband's body. There is never a good time to ring or knock! As well as *Coronation Street* and *EastEnders* to contend with, now, in the world of Sky Plus, digital TV and the internet, nobody is exactly sitting at home waiting for you to knock.

When I was first elected in 1986 it had come as a bit of a shock to Labour – and even more of a shock to me. There hadn't been a Liberal on the council for over a decade so when I turned up having defeated a Conservative nobody knew what to do with me – literally. It took half an hour to get myself into the councillors' car park as the attendant looked this fresh-faced 22-year-old up and down with the same degree of disdain as a bouncer outside a nightclub. As the only non-Tory or Labour councillor they had no idea where I should sit, or what my status was. I was not exactly breaking the mould of British politics, but I felt a combination of fear and pleasure at breaking into their cosy two-party club.

Things soon became very uncosy when the local Labour councillors had a massive falling out as the left of the party started to dominate the group. The mid-1980s were the period of internal battles in the party and Neil Kinnock watched as Eric Heffer stormed out of the Labour conference. Back in Watford a band of right-wing Labour councillors split away and created a group called 'Traditional Labour'. It was all very dramatic at the time and resulted in the remaining Labour group losing their overall majority on the council. It now became a hung council as Traditional Labour declared their intention to vote with the Conservatives. The maths were clear even to me – with my one vote I now held the balance of power. I'd been a councillor for a year and now had both sides offering everything under the sun in return for power.

The trigger for this whole showdown was a motion from the Labour left to make Nelson Mandela a freeman of Watford. Twenty years on it does not seem an unreasonable proposal, but in 1987 it became the focus of left versus right, symbolism versus common sense, and guess who had the casting vote? In the end I agreed that the issue should not be about the merits of Nelson Mandela, but more about what kind of person should become a freeman of our town. To illustrate the point I proposed that the local football manager, Graham Taylor, should be made a freeman. He had been the architect behind community football and blazed a trail by creating a family friendly ground, making the Watford team go into schools and wipe out violence. This is all commonplace now, but then it was cutting-edge stuff – and at the same time he'd dragged the team from Division Four to second place in the First Division and a cup final to boot. He was a local hero and in my judgement not a greater figure than Mandela, but more appropriate to Watford.

Of course with hindsight we can see that one went on to become known as a turnip-related disaster, the other an international statesman. However, back in 1987 the decision was tougher and I joined with the Tories to defeat the motion for Mandela's honour and was immediately branded 'Mark II Tory'. I agreed to keep the left out of power and in doing so became a hate figure for Labour. At one council meeting things became so heated that Labour supporters spat at me as I entered the chamber and threw cushions from the public gallery at me. It took me a long time to get over my hatred of the thug tendency of Labour and in a strange way it still colours my view today. Despite spit and cushion throwing I have fond memories of my eight years in that chamber. I was not alone for long and our group grew to six by the time I retired in 1994. I am very proud to say that in the decade that followed the group grew even further and, remarkably, held twenty-nine seats to take control of the council.

In 2005 I returned, now an MP, to the same council chamber to take part in a general election debate with Charles Clarke and David Davis for Channel 4. Before filming I wandered in to take a look at my old seat and suddenly found myself bursting into tears. The emotion was powerful and no doubt fuelled by election exhaustion but my researcher, Owen, had to drag me out of sight for a good few minutes to recover.

That same night we also needed more than a few moments for a different kind of recovery. I was wearing a rather old suit and the lining had split in my breast pocket. I'd popped my mobile, still on, into the pocket; now five minutes before we went live, the damn thing was ringing away lost somewhere down the back of my jacket. At first I thought I might be able to kill it by locating the off button through the material. This was quickly abandoned when I managed instead to increase the volume. Next Owen attempted keyhole surgery via the pocket, only to discover his hand could not reach the buzzing Nokia. In the end, as Jon Snow was taking his final position, we performed a satisfying rip on the inside and Caesarean-like withdrew the offending phone with seconds to spare.

I'd been a local councillor in Watford for four years and as the run-up to the 1992 election got closer it seemed the natural thing to apply to stand for the parliamentary seat when it was advertised. As I was the leader of a small group of councillors and the best known of the Liberal/SDP politicians in the area the selection was hardly a battle. The seat was a no-hoper for the party so there was little interest from other candidates. So, in November 1990, I found myself as a prospective parliamentary candidate for the first time. I was immensely proud to stand in the constituency I was born and brought up in and if I could swap my Winchester seat for Watford I would grab the chance. I love Winchester and the constituents have been wonderfully supportive through good and bad times, but to this day I have an emotional draw to Watford and when I go back for football matches I find it all very nostalgic.

And so it was that ten years after leaving school I now found myself in the odd situation of asking those old classmates to vote for me. The 1992 election campaign was not full of many dramas in Watford, but was great fun.

Belinda and I were engaged at the time of the campaign and I was delighted to have her alongside to keep my spirits up. She was, however, not always a calming influence. Campaigning with Belinda has three characteristics: shops, timekeeping and parking tickets. In Watford she managed to combine all three with remarkable regularity. Just pulling into a side street to purchase a new jumper would involve spending money, losing time and gaining the inevitable parking ticket. If we'd had to declare her parking fines as an election expense I would have been over the limit by polling day. But she saved her *pièce de résistance* till polling day itself. Now, on polling day things are pretty frantic, and elections are an all-hands-on-deck experience. Except for Belinda, who managed to combine a parking ticket with a hairdo and a flat tyre, which together seemed to tie up the agent, the candidate and half the campaign team for most of the day.

The sitting MP in Watford was that rare creature, a pro-European left-wing Tory called Tristan Garel-Jones. The Labour candidate, Mike Jackson, was from the left, a card-carrying trade unionist and local councillor. We'd crossed swords on a number of occasions in the council chamber, but relations between the three of us were friendly. Thankfully in my whole political career I've never fallen out with an opponent and can't see why some feel the need to make things so personal.

During the 1992 campaign itself the Liberal Democrats had been doing well until John Major cleverly moved the debate onto hung parliaments and proportional representation. Neil Kinnock and Paddy Ashdown ended up in a muddle over deals and pacts, leaving Major to declare that if there was a hung parliament the Liberals would put Labour into power. He described the Lib Dems as a yellow Trojan horse for Labour. It had a devastating impact. Moderate Conservative voters who'd been prepared to vote for me now feared I was a closet socialist and my posters started to be taken down. Major played a clever card and that combined with Kinnock's infamous rant at the Sheffield rally was enough to squeeze out a fourth term for the Conservatives. I came a predictable third in the election but with a respectable 10,231 votes.

Tristan Garel-Jones, Conservative	29,072	48.8%
Mike Jackson, Labour	19,482	32.7%
Mark Oaten, Liberal Democrat	10,231	17.2%
J Hywel-Davies, Green Party	566	1.0%
L Davis, Natural Law Party	176	0.3%

I remember the taxi journey home from the count in the early hours of Friday morning. Hardly anybody could believe that Britain was heading for five more years of Conservative rule. It was a desperate feeling knowing that the next chance of winning was so far away. For my part it was also the end of a chapter. I knew I would not stand again in Watford and that 1992 result was the beginning of the end of my time in my beloved home town. I had no idea if I would stand anywhere else but I knew that my next attempt at winning would have to wait for five long years – and even then a bit longer than everybody else.

2

Four counts and a wedding

I should have realised that being an MP would be a stressful job given the dramas that surrounded my election in the first place back in 1997. That involved the longest count in electoral history, the smallest majority for 100 years, a court case, a police investigation into fraud, a copycat candidate, then a record-breaking by-election and, as if that was not enough, allegations that I had tried to murder one of my opponents. Belinda used to joke at the time that it would be nice to be able to say 'Did you have a nice day at the office, darling', rather than to have to read about it and watch it on the news.

After my failure in Watford, time passed quicker than I thought it would, and in my case the five years were filled with marriage, children and a growing career as a public relations consultant. We'd moved to Hampshire to be closer to Belinda's family and against all my expectations I had been selected to fight the very Tory rural seat of Winchester.

The whole process of getting selected for Parliament is enough to put any normal human being off the idea. After deciding to leave politics in Watford I began the task of finding a new parliamentary seat. Any ambitious youngster in one of the two main parties looks out for a safe seat but that's not an option for a would-be Lib Dem MP. Instead, you look out for seats where the party is in second place and not a million votes behind the winning party. There's also the rather critical question of location. Would you really be prepared to move the whole family to Scunthorpe, say, to fight an election? (In the unlikely event anyone from Scunthorpe is bothered – I'm sorry, I've never been there, but I had to pick somewhere!)

In my case, Belinda and I agreed that the M3 corridor would act as a location guidance and in a period of a year I applied for seats in Kingston, Twickenham, Richmond, Windsor and then successfully in Winchester. The further down the M3, the worse the prospects of winning the seat. It was all very demoralising.

My attempts to win the Richmond selection ended in disaster. On the day of the hustings Belinda was going to collect a suit for me from the dry cleaners but managed to fall and fracture her leg. She turned up at the meeting in a wheelchair. The sympathy vote was not enough and I ended up without my suit or a seat!

In Kingston there were no medical disasters, just a political one. I made what people said was the best speech, but ended up with one vote. I was mortified, and as I drove home flicked on the radio only to hear the opening lines of a Take That song: 'Now I guess that it's time to give up'. I took it as a message to abandon my attempts to find a seat and went home to tell Belinda I'd had enough. Thankfully the successful Kingston candidate, Ed Davey, now the MP, was generous enough to call me a few days later. He told me that to win a seat I needed to work for weeks ahead talking to members before the hustings and urged me to keep fighting. I learnt the lesson and when the Winchester party advertised for a candidate a few months later Belinda and I managed to speak to over 400 members. This time the hustings went my way and by the summer of 1994 I'd finally found a seat.

It was a hard wrench for me to leave Watford and move to the rather remote village of Itchen Abbas a few miles outside Winchester. To this day, I remain very attached to my home town. If I bump into someone born in Watford I immediately feel a wave of nostalgia. I can remember, the first night in our new house, finding it hard to sleep in such total darkness without the familiar glow of an amber street light. My conversion from townie to country boy had started the moment I met Belinda. Her family farmed in Farleigh Wallop, a wonderful country estate south of Basingstoke close to our new home. Belinda is the youngest of five girls and the rebel in the family. Perhaps that's why she picked an SDP councillor from Watford rather than a young farmer. When I first arrived at the farm I was a source of great amusement to her family. My initiation into rural life was a real eye opener. The first event was a barn dance in a wonderful barn just opposite Belinda's house. As I was flung around whilst performing the do-si-do with her mother I could hardly have dreamt that I would marry her beautiful daughter and our wedding reception would be in the very same barn a few years later. That night any thoughts I might have had about sleeping indoors were firmly dashed and I ended up providing more entertainment trying to erect a tent in the field. Within months I had progressed to a small room off the side of the house. Known as 'the cell', all previous boyfriends of daughters had started out in this room, strategically placed at the furthest point from Belinda's room and with her parents' bedroom in between. Any midnight liaison would require two terrifying sets of squeaky wooden stairs and the need to avoid disturbing a brace of springer spaniels.

I was petrified of Belinda's family. They were all larger-than-life farmers with a set of values and outlook on life a million miles away from my upbringing. I am not sure what they made of this thin, weedy boy from Watford, but from day one I was made welcome. Of course they never missed a chance to have some fun at my expense. This would always involve an element of pain. I was asked to test electric fences with my fingers, would wake up with a dead pheasant in bed and had to quickly learn how to recite 'I'm not the pheasant plucker; I'm the pheasant plucker's son' at great speed.

As an only child I had walked into the perfect family and immediately felt the warmth of Belinda's sisters and brothers-in-law. Christmas took on a whole new meaning as the farmhouse was full of children, dogs, turkey and laughter. I had never experienced anything like it.

Life settled into a pattern of work as managing director of Westminster Public Relations. I commuted to London each day and then in the evenings did my best to campaign as the Lib Dem candidate for Winchester. When you're selected three years before an election it's a long-drawn-out battle. The odds are against you as the sitting MP has all the advantages in terms of profile and resources. I was trying to juggle a demanding job and young family and to run a campaign with few resources. I remember screaming in frustration one day as I was trying to print a press release at home only to get tangled up in wet washing and nappies that had taken over my office.

By the time the 1997 election was called my Winchester team were waiting for the off. I immediately left my office at Westminster Public Relations and hit the campaign trail. It wasn't long before events started to take a strange direction in what was to become one of the most extraordinary elections anywhere in the country. I remember the day it all started to go wrong. I was due to meet up with the local National Union of Farmers.

I hate visiting farms. It takes ages to find them on the map and the instructions always assume I have the knowledge of the local gamekeeper. 'Oh, it's very simple: turn left down the track, past Bedlam Bottom and then take a sharp right at the winter barley field.' Was that field wheat or barley? Totally lost, I grab the mobile to call for directions, only to find it lost its signal ages ago and perhaps I should not have objected to the phone mast application in the village after all! Eventually a sign to Home Farm emerges in the distance, as do two barking lurchers. I pull up as close to the farmhouse as possible, giving myself a fighting chance against the dogs. There is never anybody in so I, and the barking dogs, wander around sheds and barns, until eventually a farm hand points me to the office. This is the bit I really hate. Walking in, I am met by five farmers dressed in brown cords, check shirts and green ties. I shake their hands, which are twice the size of mine, and pretend that I had no problem finding them.

Anyway this particular spring day in 1997 we were about a week into the election campaign and I had just survived a farm grilling and was heading back to the campaign HQ. As my mobile returned to life, Ingrid

Clifford, my agent, called with some bizarre news. Now I know that name conjures up visions of a tall Swedish blonde, but in Ingrid's case, she is small with jet black hair, very British, middle class and rather bohemian. I had no hesitation at all in asking her to be my agent rather than one of the young agents that the party had put forward. She was superb at motivating the team and a first-rate campaigner, and I owe her a great deal. Ingrid has quite a high voice and today she sounded unusually high and slightly flustered. 'Mark, something has happened. The list of nominations has been published and there is a candidate called Richard Huggett standing as a Literal Democrat.'

Even with my dyslexia I figured out that this could be a problem. With just one letter differentiating the words 'liberal' and 'literal' this could cause real confusion. The same guy had stood a few years ago in the European elections and got 10,000 votes, robbing the real Liberal Democrat of a seat in the European Parliament. I bellowed instructions down the phone: call Cowley Street (party headquarters), call the returning officer, call the lawyers – can we challenge this? I think the words may have been sprinkled with a few other slightly more liberal-sounding phrases at the time.

The nomination form is quite an important document as it allows candidates to stand at an election based upon a set number of the local electorate agreeing to him or her putting their name forward. We immediately set about trying to find out who the twenty electors were who had nominated the 'Literal Democrat' to see whether they knew what they were doing, or had good reason for putting forward a copycat candidate. It soon became clear that these individuals believed they had signed a document to support a real Liberal Democrat candidate. In fact when we knocked on the first door an elderly couple said how pleased they were to see me as they had recently signed my nomination form! We immediately pointed out that they had done nothing of the sort and that they had actually signed somebody else's form and had been tricked into doing so. Would they, I asked, be prepared to come with me immediately to try and explain what had happened to the returning officer to see if there was a way in which they could have their names removed?

Time was of the essence, but the couple were elderly and the husband required a walking frame. Our plan was to speed to the returning officer's office in Winchester city centre. With only an hour to spare there was no real time for pleasantries and we quickly bundled the couple into my already cramped car, chucking the walking frame into the boot. At the time my daughter Alice was only a few months old and her baby seat was fixed into the front of the car. I didn't have time to go through the elaborate process of trying to untangle all of the complicated belts and fixtures which had taken me hours to install. So I climbed into the baby seat, crouched up with my face pressed against the windscreen, feeling rather like one of those flies that hits the windscreen on the motorway. My now rather bemused prospective constituents sat on the back seat starting to argue about who had signed the false form first, their hearing aids buzzing and the walking frame clunking around in the back. As Belinda swerved through the streets of Winchester I could tell she was already wondering why the hell she'd agreed to this standing-for-Parliament lark.

By the time we arrived at the office of the returning officer, David Cowan, Ingrid and Rodney Sabine, my local party chairman, had managed to muster up a few more individuals and we had quite a posse of local electors ready to tell the Cowan that they wished to withdraw their names from the 'Literal Democrat' nomination paper. Cowan was enormously sympathetic, but said there was no provision for doing so. Things became reasonably heated when individuals said that they did not wish to nominate the 'Literal Democrat' and made it very clear to him that they had been tricked, but the law was not on our side. Our attempt to try and have his nomination withdrawn so as to allow these individuals to nominate who they really wanted had failed, however ridiculous that may seem. I am pleased to say that a few years later this particular nonsense was resolved with stronger laws on protecting the names of parties and completing nomination forms.

Throughout the campaign I never thought there was a chance of winning. Winchester was a Conservative stronghold and had been for generations. The MP was a high-profile health minister, Gerry Malone, with a majority above 10,000. It can be soul destroying to work for years in a seat when you know deep down you'll be lucky to budge the majority by a few thousand. Nevertheless things had gone well during the campaign and when Paddy Ashdown flew in by helicopter for a street rally with a week to go I was amazed at the size of the crowd and the atmosphere. Our canvass returns were in my view totally unreliable. The data was limited and the canvassing over-optimistic. If pushed our number crunchers said it was surprisingly close, but I just didn't believe it.

Election day turned out to be the hottest of the year, sapping the energy of candidates and door-knocking party workers. I remember when Malone and I faced each other at the count; we were both red as beetroots as we compared sunburn.

By polling day as a candidate your adrenalin is pumping and you are bouncing off the walls. Some candidates take polling day easy, with a tour of all the polling stations. That's not for me; I need to do something, so shoving thousands of leaflets through letter boxes was just the therapy I needed. Mind you, it can be hazardous. Put two politicians together anywhere in the world and it's not long before the conversation will turn to battle scars of the letter box variety. I've gone over twenty years without a cut or bite, but most activists will have a horror story involving a razor-sharp snapping flap, or a Yorkshire terrier that can hurl itself at the letter box at just the sight of a finger tip.

Today, however, the heat was our enemy and by the end of the day I was shattered, burnt, covered in leaflet ink and about a stone lighter. Forget the F-plan diet; one good polling day is worth weeks of Ryvita.

I got home at about 9 p.m. and shot upstairs to have a shower and change for the count. I planned to get to the Guildhall in time for the first ballot box to open. All the party handbooks tell political agents to keep the candidate away from the count until the very last moment. It's a patronising and stupid rule, which I have ignored in all the seven counts I've been a candidate in. I want to sweat it out with everybody else and get that first glimpse of the electorate's verdict.

I grabbed a quick sandwich and decided to catch the exit poll on ITV. It was then and only then I began to think it could be close. The exit poll was remarkable. The Tories had fallen to 32 per cent of the vote; we were on 18, with Labour way ahead. In Winchester there is just no Labour vote and it would nearly all have come to me. If the Tories had collapsed then maybe, just maybe. Belinda and I drove to the count and I was desperately trying to do mental arithmetic as we travelled from our village to the city centre. Each time I calculated the figures in my mind it seemed to me there would be a thousand or so votes in it, but each time I got into a mathematical muddle and cursed my failure to engage in double maths all those Wednesday afternoons ago in the 1970s.

Counts nearly always take place in a large hall. In Winchester's case this was the Guildhall and the floor was covered in tables in a horseshoe shape, with banks of counters ready to check and count the votes. In most cases you can tell an election result before a single vote is actually counted. It's simple. Boxes arrive from around the constituency and are then opened. A visual check and count is made to determine that the number of ballots per box matches the lists of those claiming to have voted. It's during this process that you can glance at how people have voted and with little scraps of paper make calculations of how many votes you have per bundle of twenty. By about 11.00 the early boxes from the nearby city areas had arrived and were from the all-important council estates. I could hardly take in what I saw. I was getting fifteen, sixteen, sometimes seventeen votes per bundle of twenty. My heart started to pound, my team started to jump around, sharing figures in disbelief. This was way ahead of what we could have expected.

I attempted to calm things down by pointing out that the boxes from the rural areas were still arriving by car and they would be totally Tory dominated. And they were. Bit by bit, reality kicked in and village after village delivered Malone sixteen, seventeen, eighteen-plus votes per bundle.

Not a single actual vote had been counted, but in this first check of the papers it began to be clear we could be in for a long night. But even then nothing could have prepared us for just how long or the dramas that were to follow.

When all the bundles have been checked the returning officer is able to make a verification to confirm how many people have voted. This complete, the bundles are then all opened and the real count starts and each ballot paper is put in a pile for each candidate. I was starting to notice a rather large number of ballot papers going into trays for the 'Literal Democrat', Richard Huggett. It was deeply frustrating to think these were votes for me and there was nothing I could do about it. Huggett himself was the most bizarre and annoying person you could wish to meet. Tall and dressed like a 1950s cad, he looked like he could be in an Ealing comedy, but with the touch of that racing pundit, John McCririck. He was all moustache and bow tie, with a pompous public school accent. Eccentric and typically British, this buffoon was starting to get on my nerves as he strutted around saying how he had won so many votes.

The evening dragged on and on and became tenser as the two main piles for Oaten and Malone seemed to grow at the same pace on the main stage. By now it was six in the morning and I was trailing by 280 votes. Huggett marched up to me and crowed that his 600 votes had cost me the election. I totally lost control. I lurched forward and grabbed that bloody bow tie and had both my hands round his neck. I should feel ashamed, but to be honest I found it deeply satisfying. In my defence I'd been up for twenty-four hours, was physically and mentally exhausted and I was now facing defeat because this man had tricked the voters. I surprised myself as I hardly ever lose my temper and hate conflict.

A few months after the election I took a call from the chief constable for Hampshire. Huggett had decided to press charges against me for threatening to kill him. The press found out and the resulting headlines were the last thing I needed. Thankfully the police decided it was not worth pursuing and the episode ended with a friendly bit of advice from the chief constable: 'Mark, next time you try and kill somebody, can I suggest you don't do it in front of a room full of hundreds of people and with two live TV cameras on you.' He had a point.

By now it was seven in the morning. Everybody was totally exhausted and it was decided that it would be impossible to continue counting. There was also a practical problem. The Guildhall was needed for a wedding reception the next day and it had to be cleared. Democracy was put on hold and as we were heading for our fourth recount it was agreed this would be moved to a new venue at 2.00 p.m. on Friday. Suddenly

Screwing Up

Winchester was set to become the longest count in history and due to the arrangements of an unknown bride and groom the media gave my election the nickname of 'Four Counts and a Wedding'!

This was unprecedented. Counts don't get stopped mid-way through. I'd never known anything like this and was deeply worried that the votes of 70,000 people would now be bundled up and moved to a new location. I was emotionally and physically shattered and to leave the Guildhall without knowing the result was a massive blow. Belinda and I walked out in the emerging daylight and people told us to try and get some rest. As if I would be able to just go home and sleep when the result of my life was on hold – suspended between becoming a member of Parliament and remaining managing director of a public relations consultancy.

As we drove home my phone was buzzing with family and friends trying to find out what was going on. The Teletext service just had Winchester down as 'no result', now, apart from the Northern Ireland ones, the only seat not to have declared. I remember my father calling from Italy. 'Well, why have you not called about what happened?'

'I don't know yet, Dad.'

'What do you mean, you don't know?'

'Well, we've all gone home and will start again later today,' I tried to explain. As the words came out they didn't sound that convincing; I was sure my dad must think this was some elaborate cover-up to avoid telling him I'd lost.

I switched the television on when I got in and watched those amazing images of Tony Blair addressing the Labour Party faithful and the powerful image of a new day, era, dawn, all emerging. That rare moment in politics when you sense an energy and change for good. At the same time I checked out the results of my political generation. Ed Davey had made it in Kingston, just, by fifty-six votes, and others who'd been on training weekends with me over the years had now fulfilled their dreams as the Liberal Democrat Parliamentary Party rose to forty-five. But as the morning dragged on I still had no idea if I would be taking that number up to forty-six. I just about managed to take a shower and get forty winks before we headed off to the Guildhall for the second part of the count.

It was another hot day in Winchester and by now word had spread to the national media that something very unusual was going on there. As we arrived at the Guildhall I chatted to some of the journalists and then headed for a team meeting to discuss how we would handle this final count. Our main problem was exhaustion. The Lib Dem team of counting monitors was in no fit state to scrutinise the count. Normally a counting agent's work is not so vital, but with arguments developing over each ballot paper we needed a fresh, alert team to check as every vote was counted. Thankfully Rodney Sabine had managed to track down some back-ups at party HQ in London. When he put in his 'Houston, we've got a problem' call there was little interest amongst the partying HQ staff, until eventually, as the prospect of winning an extra seat emerged, one of the national team, Candy Piercy, drove to Winchester with a fresh team of young activists. We were organised and alert as the new count started in a small committee room at the very top of the Guildhall.

Meanwhile, to our relief and slight amusement, the Conservative team seemed to have stuck with the blue rinse grannies who had been up all night. You could see them struggling to keep their eyes open. The heat was unbearable in the room and there was to be no relief from air fans because they had to be turned off after they blew loads of ballot papers off the table. So, bit by bit, in sweltering conditions, every single ballot paper was held up to a light, checked to see if it had the official mark and then placed in either an Oaten box or a Malone box.

This went on and on throughout the afternoon. My secretary at Westminster Public Relations kept calling for updates. 'What do I do with next week's meetings?'

'I've no idea, sorry.'

As we drew towards late afternoon, David Cowan called Malone and me over. The piles of ballots on the table were so close that we both had absolutely no idea by looking at the hundreds of bundles all stacked up. I saw Cowan holding a piece of paper and desperately tried to read the figures but his shaking hands made it blur just as I was about to make it out. He then told us that I had 26,100 votes to Malone's 26,098: I had a two-vote lead. I assumed that Malone would call for a further count but he just shrugged his shoulders and immediately conceded to me. My mind was racing, unable to take it all in. I seem to remember telling Ingrid and Belinda but apart from that the room was virtually empty. Then Mrs Malone suddenly rushed up to me and said: 'Do you realise what you've done? You have ruined a political career. Because of you we will have to see the bank manager on Monday!'

I was a bit taken aback, but managed to mutter how sorry I was. Ironically, I suspect in the years that followed I was the one that needed to see bank managers and Malone's finances will have improved greatly away from the world of politics.

During the afternoon count word had got out that something strange was going on in Winchester. By six o'clock a very large crowd had gathered outside the steps of the Guildhall, spilling into the street in such numbers that the police had to shut the road. The good folk of Winchester wanted to know why they were the last constituency in the country to get a member of Parliament. The returning officer decided to give them what they wanted and declare the result outside on the balcony overlooking the city centre under the watchful eye of King Alfred's statue a few feet away. With live TV waiting for the drama to unfold, Belinda and I stepped onto the balcony keeping straight faces. I am not sure why I didn't just run out and shout 'I've won!', but I am told I should take up cards as my poker face convinced people I'd lost. Malone always looked miserable so there was little clue from his expression. As the results were read out it took a second or two for the crowd to figure it out – then an enormous roar went up and I was able to smile, kiss Belinda and then say a few words. It was a wonderful moment and an incredible release of nerves after the events of the last twenty-four hours. Within minutes the police asked me to move away from the city centre to help clear the road.

'How do I do that?' I asked.

'Sir, basically, if you move then the crowd will follow you.'

And they did, to the grounds of the cathedral, and as the sun set we held a celebration surrounded by bemused journalists, voters and supporters. It was unbelievable. I'd survived the longest count in history, won the smallest majority in a century and was now member of Parliament for this great city of Winchester. I could hardly take it all in. But the moment was not to last long. This bizarre election was to take yet another dramatic twist.

Within about an hour of the declaration, journalists started to tell me that the Malone camp was going to try and challenge the result. It was devastating news and any joy quickly turned to fear. What else could happen? We badly needed time to decide what to do next and knew that the Conservatives were desperate to act fast and serve me with a writ to try and get the election declared void. Word got out that the legal firm acting for Malone was trying to track me down to serve the notice. Somehow I had to get from Winchester to a meeting with our lawyers in London without being spotted. The Monday after polling day Rodney Sabine picked me up and we caught the Basingstoke train to Waterloo. Things were looking good as we travelled in a cab to the party HQ in Cowley Street. As the cab drew up some guy was lurking by the front door so Rodney pushed me onto the floor of the cab, covering with me a coat, and went over to check out the stranger. The poor chap turned out to be a window cleaner so, panic over, we picked up the party chief executive, Chris Rennard, and headed to the City offices of my legal team.

In the swanky reception I eased back in a chair and glanced across at a drop-dead gorgeous girl. To my surprise she looked back and said: 'Are you Mark Oaten?' I confirmed I was, surprised and a bit flattered to be recognised, only for her to stand up, march over and hand me an envelope with a writ from the Tories! That'll teach me to smile at pretty ladies!

Once the legal process began there were endless potential outcomes with plenty of twists and turns along the way. The legal teams had plenty to argue over. The biggest debate was over fifty-five ballot papers that had not got the official electoral mark on them. The Malone camp's case rested on an assumption that if these had been included he would have won. Nobody was 100 per cent sure just what was on the fifty-five votes but my team felt from what they could remember at the count that I did not have that many of them. After months of argument the court and both parties agreed that the fifty-five papers should be examined and counted. Both sides gathered in a room in central London and a judge began to open each paper and announce if they showed a cross for Oaten or Malone. If I'd got a majority of these I think Malone would have given up his fight for a recount. Bit by bit the papers were called out and to my surprise it was running neck and neck until at the last moment Malone edged ahead by just four votes. Enough to turn my majority of two into a majority of two for him, if the fifty-five papers were allowed to be included.

It was a key turning point and now meant Malone felt he had a moral victory. Of course it was not that clear; with the 'Literal Democrat' gaining over 600 votes I felt an even stronger claim to the moral victory. The whole period was enormously unsettling and made my first few months harder than normal for a new MP. Everybody at Westminster knew that my future was uncertain. Was I there by fault, a fraud that would soon be gone? You could see the officials pointing at 'the guy with two votes'.

The uncertainty also had a financial impact. Before the election I had been a director of Westminster Public Relations, a successful public affairs and PR consultancy. I owned shares and at the time the company was about to float on the stock market, which would have given me a nice profit. However, the rules on MPs' links with public affairs consultancies are very clear – you are not allowed to have any financial interest, so although I faced the prospect of being thrown out as an MP within weeks of my election I had no choice but to resign from my job and sell my shares.

The only positive during this uncertainty was the reaction of my new constituents. The local newspaper and regional TV had been carrying the unfolding court drama each night and I had become an easily recognised figure when I walked around Winchester. Throughout the summer of 1997 Belinda and I could not go anywhere without a constant stream of people, all with a story to tell about how their two votes had made the difference. Stories of people leaving hospital and making last-minute dashes to the polling station became commonplace. 'It was our two votes' was the common cry and there were even badges printed saying 'I am one of the two'. The most welcome comments were from those Conservatives who had not voted for me but typically declared: 'I am a Tory but want you to know it's just not cricket to challenge the result. You deserve a chance to prove yourself.'

I soon began to realise just how strongly people felt about this. As the national media, lawyers and party leaders argued away, deep down I knew what the mood was locally – all I needed now was the chance to fight the election again, and I sensed I would romp home.

My only fear was that the courts would try to reverse the election and refuse a rerun. By the end of July things were starting to come to a head and both sides were called to a critical hearing and judgment at the Old Bailey. The scene felt like a murder trial as I battled my way through a throng of cameras and microphones into the court. The hearing seemed to take ages as we rehearsed the whole history of the case. Malone was just a few seats ahead of me as we both awaited the outcome. I would have been mortified if the judge ruled that Malone had won and began to fear the outcome. Eventually he ruled the election was void and should be rerun. Although it meant I was no longer an MP I was relieved – I had a chance to put my case again. I made sure I got out of court first to do interviews, eager to show that far from being down or dejected I welcomed the chance to run again and let the people of Winchester decide. All that remained was for the Speaker to announce that I was no longer an MP, which she duly did when Parliament returned in early October. It was a historic moment. There are not many MPs thrown out in this way and it marked the end of the court phase before we moved into a by-election.

At home things were not great. Belinda and I had a young baby, Alice, and I was now out of a job, having given up my directorship and having been thrown out as an MP. All of this had been played out in the national media and we'd lost any privacy as we went out or to the shops. We'd try to have a row in Homebase about paint colour only for somebody to intervene to offer a view on the two votes. As a young family we'd been waiting to make all sorts of plans for the future until after the outcome of the election; now I had to persuade Belinda to hang on a bit longer for our life to be resolved. I guess it's hardly surprising that during this period I was also trying to deal with a load of stupid stress-related stuff. Aches and pains in my chest freaked me out and I was on all sorts of beta blockers to try and calm things down. I'd never wanted this to happen; I'd imagined I would lose Winchester gracefully and go back to work. Now I found my life turned upside down, short of money and not sure what the future held.

As the party began the build up to the by-election a few more twists took place. The police announced that they wanted to investigate the election because of claims of electoral fraud. With such a focus on the close result it emerged that four voters had turned up to vote at their polling stations only to be told that somebody had already voted under their name. At the time the four were asked to vote on a special red ballot paper which is set aside. I guess this is normally just lost in the system but with the close result these four voters let it be known that they felt robbed of their vote and the police started to investigate. At one point there was even talk of opening up all the ballot papers again to withdraw the impersonators' votes and replace them with the four red papers filled in by the genuine voters. This was another twist that could have changed the result. In the end the police investigation resulted in two prosecutions and an accountant was actually charged and barred from practice under electoral fraud laws.

Then came the most helpful of twists. At every election a marked register is kept which records who actually voted and this is released six months after the election and made a public document. My local party obtained a copy and we could not believe it when we discovered that Malone and his wife had not voted in the Winchester election. Their votes had been cast in Aberdeen, a marginal seat, as they had decided Winchester was safe enough for them not to bother. Bingo! The press had a field day when they reported that his two-vote loss was because he and his wife had not voted. I could not believe my luck. It all helped ink the image that Malone was an absent MP. Jokes began to emerge around the city. 'What's the difference between Mark Oaten's and Gerry Malone's homes? – Mark Oaten's has furniture in it.' With this news the stage was well and truly set for a rerun and a titanic battle between the parties. The date was set for 20 November and the campaigning got under way.

By-elections are odd political occasions; normally caused by the death of an MP, they become a mini general election and a chance to test the political mood. In my case I most certainly had not died and the political mood was still firmly with Labour just six months after their landslide victory. There was no real national issue and unlike some by-elections this was never going to be a referendum on, say, the poll tax or the war in Iraq. That said, the Lib Dems wanted to hang onto their forty-sixth seat and the Tories were desperate for some good news – that meant the streets and villages of the constituency were full of activists from across the country and the Westminster press were more than happy to spend a week in the countryside enjoying village pubs and the newly opened Hotel du Vin. Indeed it is rumoured that our party election guru, Chris Rennard, only agreed to concede the Tories' legal challenge after he'd checked out the various restaurants and hotels in the area.

With the circus in town, Belinda and I found the atmosphere very different from the way we'd campaigned in the general election. Then a small team had been pushed hard but had made all the decisions, now the national party was calling the shots. Despite this I was determined to keep some control. I knew that thousands of Conservatives wanted to vote for me to show Malone he was wrong to challenge the result. Why put them off with lots of Lib Dem messages and attacks on the Tories? I wanted this to be a very local election based on my early record as an MP and the sense of fair play. I was also concerned to hear that Paddy Ashdown had discussed the election with Tony Blair – there had been talk of Labour giving me an easy ride. With Labour getting just 6,000 votes at the election they agreed there was no chance of winning but if their voters tactically backed me it would help. Nevertheless I was confident I could win alone and if the Conservatives got wind that Labour were backing me it would be a nightmare – I would be portrayed as a Labour Trojan horse. No thanks!

Day one of the campaign began with the arrival of my minder/driver, Alex Faulkes. In the next five weeks we were hardly separated and the family became very fond of this quietly spoken but rock-solid guy who always calmed me down and had my interests at heart. However, things did not start well. Alex turned up on Monday and I dutifully handed him my car keys after I was told I would not be allowed to drive until the election was over. We got into the car and Belinda came out to wave us off.

Then Alex proceeded to reverse the car over Pepper, our springer spaniel. We both heard the thud and jumped out to find thankfully that, springer by name and by nature, he had bounced off the car. It broke the ice and provided an entertaining story for weeks ahead. I hated being driven, particularly as Alex decided he would drive everywhere at about 10 mph below the speed limit and I felt like some kind of regal tortoise. My only real falling out with Alex was my constant screaming to get a move on.

As the days turned into weeks I soon got into the by-election routine: three canvass sessions a day and a Lib Dem MP visiting for a photo shoot. If you had the agriculture spokesman down then you would head off to a farm for an hour, welly boots covered in mud, do an interview and then that was it. Health spokesman – off to the hospital, home affairs – the police. I think you get the general idea. Often the media would mic me and the MP up and it took all my discipline to avoid swearing or telling Lembit Öpik to shut up as we were being filmed. From memory it seemed to rain solidly for four weeks, creating nightmares trying to juggle umbrellas, canvass cards and steamed-up car windows. The whole thing was a slog but Paddy Ashdown and the party really came through for me. Ashdown was 100 per cent behind me and visited on numerous occasions, as did party activists from all over the UK who gave up their weekend to support the campaign. The biggest boost, however, was the response of voters. Each canvass session was incredible with virtually every person saying they would vote for me – a unique experience that I've never had before or since. I know how Putin felt.

Unlike in May, this time the result was never in question. The local community had decided that Malone was a bad loser and they wanted to give me a chance to carry on. The support was overwhelming from council estate to country estate. Head Office kept repeating that it was going to be close, to keep everybody on their toes, but I knew what people were saying to me in such large numbers. As I insisted on canvassing I knew what the scores were each night – so I was not so anxious as I turned up to the Guildhall for the by-election count on 20 November. The Oaten bundles grew and grew. In some areas we were getting eighteen out of twenty votes, an incredible sight for anybody who has watched election counts.

Eventually at about one in the morning I walked onto the stage and the result was read out. I am dyslexic and get into a bit of a muddle trying to figure out my majority – initially I thought it was 12,000 but in fact was 21,556. In the end I had 37,006 compared to Malone's 15,450. It was one of the highest number of votes ever for an MP in Great Britain.

I wasn't the only person to muddle up the result. When Paddy Ashdown was called at midnight he barked at Chris Rennard: 'No, not his number of votes, I want his majority.'

'Paddy, 22,000 *is* his majority,' Rennard proudly announced.

From a majority of 2 to 22,000 in six months is a wonderful response from the people of Winchester. I was incredibly moved and grateful and to this day will never forget how a whole community decided their young MP deserved a second chance.

My journey from Watford to Winchester finally ended in Westminster and a few days later I took my place on the green benches this time sure that nobody could challenge my election and assuming naively that the dramas in my political life were a thing of the past.

3

It shouldn't happen to an MP

After the most dramatic of starts, life at Westminster started to settle into a pattern of sorts, but the job has never been normal. The weeks rush by in a blur of speeches, emails and solving problems in a world which lurches from farce to exhaustion.

My work is divided between Winchester and Westminster and I've learned to live a Jekyll-and-Hyde existence. In Westminster events are out of my hands as government whips, the media and old-fashioned parliamentary protocol set the agenda. Thankfully in Winchester I'm more in charge about how to decide what kind of constituency MP I want to be. I have held a weekly surgery in my constituency for the last twelve years. After a while you immediately know if you are going to be able to help somebody, or if your role is to be a sympathetic listener. The surgeries can be highly charged. People are often at their wits' end and it's quite common for them to break down in tears, which often triggers me to join in. My first aim is to try and put people at their ease, dispelling any nervousness they might have over visiting an MP. I insist I am called Mark and we have a cupboard full of toys for young children to play with so parents can chat away without distraction.

Of course things are not always pleasant and occasionally people get angry. Sadly some years ago my colleague Nigel Jones, then MP for

Cheltenham, was attacked with a knife and his agent, Andrew Pennington, was killed. Thankfully I've never felt unsafe. Our own rather pathetic safety measure is a can of air freshener spray. Anybody messing with us will get an eyeful of pine forest – very Winchester!

Each Friday I am joined in surgery by Joan Read, a bespectacled retired doctor. She has seen over 3,000 cases with me over the years. Together we listen, write notes and suppress our tears and laughter and our views as best we can.

Cases swing from serious to irritating. One moment you're trying to console a widow and help with her pension; the next, two neighbours are arguing over four inches of gravel drive. It can be very frustrating. I just about avoid telling the latter kind of people to get a life, but at the end of the day they pay my salary as an MP and when you win your first election by just two votes it does make you pay attention to everybody. Well, almost. There are some people beyond help. Mr Jones was a regular at surgery until we put him on our blacklist. A scruffy, small fifty-year-old, with a Michael Foot-style donkey jacket, he first turned up with a rather peculiar request. 'Mr Oaten, would you look at my testicle please?'

'No, certainly not.'

'I think you should, it's a matter of importance,' he insisted.

'Well, I'm sorry, although this is a surgery, it's not that kind of surgery.'

'Well, it is a matter of national security, then. Now will you look?'

'No! But out of interest, why?'

'MI5 have planted a probe into one testicle and I think you should see it.'

I remember telling this story to a group of civil servants I was training on what it's like to be an MP. The anecdote normally gets a laugh, but on this occasion the group was in hysterics as the talk was also being signed. The sign for 'testicles' was indeed rather peculiar and merited repeating the story for another look.

I had a similar request to examine the same body part from another constituent a few years later, this time because a dog had bitten him in that particular area. Fortunately he was persuaded to send in photographs. It was clear the dog had not given up easily.

Screwing Up

The intelligence services tend to get the blame for a fair bit. Strange bumps, noises, visions and movements are regularly the subject of constituents' complaints. A Mr Smith, however, took this to new extremes. He refused to give details of why he wished to see me, other than that it was a matter of the utmost importance and highly confidential. When his time came he plonked a bag of bathroom tiles on the desk in front of me and insisted I read a letter he wanted me to deliver to the Home Secretary. The letter told that Mr Smith's nasal hair was highly sensitive and had been picking up secret security codes in the early hours of the morning, causing him sleepless nights. The week before at 4.30 a.m. half a dozen tiles had fallen off his bathroom wall as a result of these secret codes beaming in via his nose. This explained the tiles in the Tesco bags, or as they were now known, exhibit A.

I've also had my fair share of people claiming to have seen extra-terrestrials and on one occasion a request to meet with aliens. I immediately called my diary secretary and asked her to set a date for the constituent to fix up the meeting. It seemed to do the trick and he left happy. I'm still waiting!

Like the members of any profession MPs have a black humour and we deal with these kinds of bizarre cases as best we can. I remember one of my colleagues, the Isle of Wight MP Dr Peter Brand, saying that he still ran his doctor's surgery on Monday morning and MP's surgery on Friday. It often occurred to him that people were actually attending the wrong one.

The most frustrating cases are when young couples have clearly got together and had children far too early. I don't say this from any moral outrage, just sadness that the opportunity and ambition of youth is snatched away and all too often I see them looking exhausted, angry and desperate.

Every now and then some people turn up and tell a tale that is so moving you are spurred into action. About a year after I was first elected a tall, very dignified, elderly gentleman came into surgery for his allotted fifteen minutes. His name was Keith Martin. Half an hour later I was mesmerised by his recollections of being held as a prisoner of war in Japan. The combination of bravery, alongside brutality, was hard to grasp in the comfort of my Winchester office. Mr Martin had two simple demands. He and his fellow PoWs wanted an apology from Japan and compensation for their time in captivity. After all Japan was now one of the world's richest nations and sought to be welcomed as a civilised country on the international stage. In return Mr Martin felt it was little to ask.

I decided to spring into action and the next week at Westminster went about establishing a cross-party group to campaign for the apology and £10,000 compensation for each PoW. It was the start of a two-year battle and the opportunity to work alongside a group of survivors and heroes who I learnt a great deal from. Working with lawyers, the media and fellow politicians, I used all my old lobbying skills and quickly learned that the pressure created away from the floor of the House was more important than endless debates. Eventually we were successful and the government agreed to a compensation programme. It was my first success at Westminster and to this day is one of the very few things I can point to where I feel I've made a difference.

One other occasion came towards the end of 1998 when I decided to put my name in the ballot for a private member's bill. It's a total lottery as the names of twenty MPs are drawn out and given the chance to introduce their own law. I was drawn number six, high enough to stand a very real chance of finding parliamentary time to get a law passed.

Within seconds of the ballot being announced my office was bombarded with suggestions for legislation from all the major charities with their pet projects. As an MP in this situation you have two options: go for a massively controversial issue which will get plenty of coverage but stands no chance of becoming law, or pick something that might just pass the numerous hurdles. I chose the latter route and took the unusual path of going to see the Labour government whips to find out if they had any new bills they'd not yet had time to introduce. I selected three and then decided to be a bit radical and via the local newspaper asked my constituents to pick which of the three they wanted. In the end a local couple motivated hundreds of people to back one of the ideas, a bill to reform adoption from overseas countries. It turned out that two of my constituents, Clive and Beth Houghton, had already adopted children from abroad and had become experts in the problems with the current law. Thanks to their lobbying I picked the Inter-Country Adoption Bill and I am pleased to say that a year later it became law.

Taking a private member's bill through gave an insight into how Parliament really works. The key to a backbench bill becoming law is to get the government on board (which I'd done by selecting a draft government bill), but it also required skill and luck with the Friday morning awkward squad. Private member's bills are debated on a Friday, when most MPs are back in their constituencies. This makes it very easy for a few MPs to block a bill by just talking away until it runs out of time. The master at this craft was the colourful Tory MP Eric Forth. In effect on Fridays he acted like a Roman emperor, giving the thumbs up or down to any bill by the length at which he spoke. Deciding on a direct path, I sought out Eric for a meeting. I explained that my bill aimed to stop the illegal trafficking of children for sale and would also help to speed up adoption for genuine couples who went through the proper processes. He was polite, listened, raised questions and then declared that because I'd been decent enough to explain things to him, my bill would have his support.

When the Friday came I was petrified at having to introduce a bill and was constantly looking to my right to see if Eric would jump up and change his mind. Thankfully, he was true to his word and due to his agreement and the commitment of the Houghtons, I am pleased to have played my part in helping to stop the disgrace of children being sold and then hidden in car boots to smuggle them into the UK. Sadly, Eric Forth and Clive Houghton have since died.

The new law was not without its critics, particularly those that objected to the idea of foreign children being adopted into this country. I began to get some nasty letters from racist groups and then eventually a number of death threats from a group called Combat 18. The threats were rather specific, saying that they knew where I lived and threatening my family. I was alarmed and told the House of Commons Security Authority, who immediately made contact with the police in Hampshire. For a few months we had to keep an eye out, check under the car and put some security measures in place at home. It was not too much of a problem, but unfortunately coincided with the birth of our second daughter, Milly. On police advice Belinda was asked to stay in a room hidden at the back of the maternity ward at Royal Hampshire County Hospital, Winchester, rather than a new suite in the maternity unit. It was annoying that politics got in the way of Milly's birth, but to be honest, I was in much more of a panic about watching her being born than any threat from Combat 18.

Milly was born via a planned caesarean, giving me plenty of time to get nervous about the operation. Belinda is amazing at hospital and remained totally calm as I got into a terrible muddle, trying to put the sterile blue shoe covers over my head by mistake. I felt decidedly sick and faint as they started to cut into Belinda's stomach and had to be escorted out by a couple of nurses who must have thought I was a total wimp – and would have been right. I eventually recovered in time to see Milly being pulled out. As Belinda recovered I had this wonderful hour alone with my baby girl, but I immediately noticed that something was wrong with her feet as they both bent inward. I hoped they would just spring round to normal, but in the end we discovered she had talipes or club foot and that it would take several operations over the year ahead to put her right. It's a horrid experience to have to take your baby to undergo surgery. In our case it was minor and all fine, but the experience taught me just how lucky we've been with our children – it left me with everlasting respect for those parents with seriously ill children that need regular hospital care.

Of course an MP's surgery is not all fun and games and the most moving of cases are those involving medical problems. One of my earliest involved a woman who arrived to see me in a wheelchair, suffering from motor neurone disease. Her life expectancy, like anybody with this cruel disease, was not long. Bit by bit she was being paralysed from the waist upwards. She'd heard of a new drug that was said to slow down, or in some cases halt, the disease. I felt an enormous responsibility as I went into battle with government ministers to try and get this drug available on the NHS. Each week you are dealing with people waiting for hip replacements, heart by-passes and other new drugs. In Hampshire there is a particular policy to limit IVF treatment and to this day I am campaigning on behalf of a number of couples to have age restrictions removed so they don't have to wait until thirty-six for their first chance of treatment.

Some of the stories you hear are terribly upsetting. The child of one of my constituents was murdered by the father, who then killed himself. Overnight she lost her husband and child. I could only offer a hug and tissues in response.

Over the years you start to spot the signs of depression and stress in constituents. I guess there is a danger that you become an amateur shrink; a little knowledge is a dangerous thing, but I always ensure that I speak to the constituent's doctor or the local mental health team if I am in any doubt about someone's mental state. Constituents will occasionally just collapse and break down, shaking and hugging me.

It's frightening and upsetting to see people out of control in this way. I hug back and then try to get them to consider getting help for their depression. I often advocate Prozac or an anti-depressant. I've no training or right to suggest this other than my own experience. It's meant to be a taboo subject to admit taking an anti-depressant. I am not sure why this is the case. I see it as a sign of somebody that is trying to get help and resolve some problems. Matched with counselling and other techniques it can be a helpful prop during difficult times.

I've taken two courses of anti-depressants: firstly when I was stressed and unhappy during my time as home affairs spokesman and then again in the weeks following my scandal – but more of that later. I admire both David Blunkett and Alastair Campbell for admitting to their depressions. It shows you can be successful at work and depressed at the same time – it's just not a great idea!

Unlike many inner-city MPs I don't have a massive immigration workload. I remember being asked on *Any Questions* if I would require Arab women to remove their burkas in surgery (Jack Straw had declared the week before that he did). I responded jokingly that in Winchester I was more likely to ask constituents to remove a Prada scarf than anything else. But immigration issues and in particular human rights issues have become a cause I've regularly taken up away from Winchester.

Some of the most moving and upsetting experiences I've seen have been on parliamentary visits abroad. The death cells that I saw in St Vincent were awful. When we were on an official tour there was this moment when the prison governor started talking to the visiting MPs. We all went silent, listening to his every word, and at that moment a massive cockroach ambled across from the cell towards the governor's shoes. He stopped talking, paused, looked down and, as six pairs of parliamentary eyes watched, he promptly stamped on the insect and continued as if nothing had happened.

The cells and conditions were truly like a living hell. Prisoners could not stand up and just crouched like animals in an unfit zoo. We were shown the gallows, which were on top of the prison. A condemned man reaches them via a stairway which leads from the cells through to the roof of the prison and the last thing a prisoner sees before his neck is broken is the most amazing Caribbean blue sea. It is an image which still haunts me today.

During the visit I looked in at the workshop to see some of the inmates, dressed in their blue prison gear, making cricket bats. One guy caught my attention as he was sanding down a bat; I showed an interest and chatted to him for some time. A couple of days later the governor called the delegation's hotel and said that this particular prisoner wanted me to have the fully finished and varnished bat. I was greatly moved and the bat has pride of place in my office. It's a horrid thought but I never found out if he was executed. My opposition to the death penalty is one of the few political issues that really motivate me and I regret not doing more in my time at Westminster to support Amnesty and other groups in their campaigns to abolish capital punishment. It is for me a great disappointment that the United States, the most powerful nation in the world, still uses a form of punishment which is not fit for this century.

The visit to St Vincent was extraordinary not just for the prison, but because it gave me a chance to see first hand the plight of Caribbean banana growers. The UK delegation was taken in a rather clapped-out minibus up to some banana plantations. The conditions were muggy and I found myself on the receiving end of a verbal and almost physical attack from one farmer. With his long dreadlocked hair and a strong smell of alcohol and cannabis he lectured me, arms waving above my head, on how the western world and American-grown bananas were killing his livelihood. These small hill-based farmers certainly can't compete with the so-called 'dollar banana regime'.

About ten years before this visit I'd ended up with Fyffes and Geest as clients when my PR agency ran the Caribbean Banana Exporter Association. It was a fun client and I even had a banana hotline on my desk. The serious part was to try and lobby the EU to help support these smaller producers. It involved one of my more bizarre activities – to present John Major with a bunch of bananas at Downing Street. Things went badly wrong when the company delivered not one bunch, but a whole bloody treeful of bananas. We needed a pick-up truck to take them to Downing Street and, not surprisingly, were refused entry. In the end we quite happily delivered them to Great Ormond Street Hospital and I think they had a bit more fun with them than John and Norma would have had.

Not all trips abroad involve deprivation. When I was asked to join a cross-party delegation to Dubai I jumped at the chance. I've never visited a country with such a 'can do' approach. Desperate to find long-term alternatives to oil, the ruling royal family has turned the city into a tourist Mecca in the space of a decade. The Crown Prince spent a considerable amount of time personally showing us how he'd achieved this. As he flew us across the city in his private helicopter he would point to a new building and tell how he had instructed the developer to just get on with it, with not a single mention of planning guidelines or a public enquiry.

The scale of development was enormous. We flew over the sea and stared down as enormous dredgers drew out sand from the sea bed to create the now famous Palm Island. The effect from the air was breathtaking as the leaves of each palm began to spring luxurious homes, fit even for the Beckhams. Later in the Crown Prince's boardroom we looked at scale drawings of his plans to recreate a miniature planet Earth in the sea, offering the wealthy the chance to buy countries. Imagine having the kind of money to play a real-life game of world Monopoly. 'Shall we buy Italy, darling?' 'No, odd shape.' 'How about Ireland then? It's nice and round.' The highlight of this chopper tour was a couple of astonishing flights round the world's first seven-star hotel, the Burj al-Arab. We could see our reflections in the dark mirrored windows of what must have been the penthouse suites.

At one point the Prince landed close to a Bedouin tribe surrounded by camels in the middle of the desert. As we went over to say hello one of them rushed off to milk a camel and before too long we were all sipping from a bucket. I am a strictly pasteurised kind of guy and therefore gulped as fast as possible, hoping to bypass my sensitive taste buds. To my amazement the Prince explained that despite their nomadic appearance the Bedouins were probably all millionaires. The royal family has been smart in ensuring the whole population has benefited from the riches of oil.

The Crown Prince was clearly into his toys. On our first day he'd managed to soak us all on a power boat trip across the bay in Dubai. He was, however, not simply a royal playboy. Educated at Eton, his English was perfect and he was keen to engage with us in a serious debate about the international terrorist situation and the oil price crisis. The United Arab Emirates borders Iraq and Iran, creating a west-friendly country in an otherwise hostile environment. The purpose behind our visit was a charm offensive from the royal family to demonstrate its willingness to help capture terrorists in the region. The Prince offered us an evening discussion on world affairs, but rather than turn up at a stuffy palace, or private hotel room, we received instructions to rendezvous in the middle of the desert for a display of his prowess with eagles. An entourage of black limos picked us up and as day turned to night we arrived at an enormous tent, literally in the middle of the desert. What appeared to be pigeons were then sent up in a mini balloon to be released on the command of what I guess was the equivalent of a gamekeeper, although the dress was white robe rather than Barbour. As the pigeons saw freedom in sight the Prince's eagles shot into the air and after a bit of squealing and feathers flying about we all politely clapped the killing in a slightly disapproving, but not wishing to offend, kind of way.

Screwing Up

We were then summoned to the tent and each allocated our own cushion. As night truly set in so did the Crown Prince and he began to deliver a three-hour lecture on the politics of the Middle East without a joke, breath, or opportunity for questions in sight. To say I had pins and needles doesn't do the agony justice. The mental pain of trying to concentrate, coupled with the loss of all sensations in the lower half of my body, was only matched by the ever-growing sensation that my bladder was about to burst. As the talk proceeded various servants plied us with more and more herbal tea and by now I was trying to work out how I could diplomatically sneak to the back of the tent to relieve myself. Eventually, and with a sudden clap of hands, the whole event concluded and four British members of Parliament stretched their limbs and rushed to the limos. We each had a car to ourselves and as the Prince departed in his helicopter, our convoy gradually moved through the desert heading for the city. Thankfully I was not the only honourable member with a bursting bladder. Word spread amongst the officials and drivers and within a few moments the fleet of cars pulled over allowing the four of us to rush into the desert for a comfort break. What utter relief, until midway through we heard the sound of the Prince's helicopter coming over the ridge and heading, lights blazing, right over the line of cars and official delegation, all watering the sand. It was the last vision the Prince had of his British visitors.

Every now and then there is a visit or event that sticks with you for life. Visiting the Holocaust Museum in Tel Aviv left me in tears, but also with a greater understanding of the bitterness of Israelis and their determination to protect their state. Every part of my visit either surprised or shocked me. In Bethlehem I could just wander into the birthplace of Christ in an abandoned square without a single sign or visitor around. In Tel Aviv I enjoyed the richness of a sunset whilst walking along the beach – in any other country a tourist haven, but here, with the risk of bombings, there wasn't a beach chair in sight. Then we went to a meeting with the PLO and visited the settlements in Gaza, communities made out of concrete tunnels with homes created from the spaces between large boulders and children running around shouting 'Manchester United!' when they saw us walking past. They seemed strangely happy in this world, perhaps because despite the horror, it was a genuine community with brothers, uncles, nephews and nieces forming strong family units.

I left the country optimistic, having spoken to politicians involved in the Bill Clinton/Ehud Barak talks at the turn of the century. Sadly, Clinton ran out of time and a decade later it may now be left to his wife to find a way forward.

In the years ahead I went on many trips abroad, mostly just with fellow MPs, but on some occasions Belinda was able to come along. It was good to have a soulmate to share the experiences, although her presence did not always lead to plain sailing. In September 2001 we'd both decided to join a delegation led by the feisty Labour MP Ann Clwyd, in conjunction with Save the Children, to Burkina Faso, the third poorest country in the world. After an uneventful stop in the Ivory Coast we flew to Bamako, in the rather fragile country of Mali, for a fuel stop before our final flight to Ouagadougou, the capital. Our stopover was at a small military airport. As we were allowed out on the tarmac Belinda went heading off on her own and when it came time to reboard I could not find her anywhere. To be honest she's always late for flights so I am more than used to getting on the plane alone. This time, however, as I looked out of the window down onto the tarmac I was alarmed to see Belinda being held by two enormous Idi Amin-type characters in full military dress. Arms were flying around and what appeared to be her camera was being tugged back and forth. Fortunately Tony Colman, the then MP for Putney, marched up and appeared to calm things down, allowing a rather sheepish Belinda to join our flight, now aware that photos and airports in Africa don't go together.

Ouagadougou itself was appalling. Terrible poverty, begging, vultures flying overhead the whole time and awful accommodation. We were staying in the Hotel Splendid, proving that the grander the name of any hotel the worse it is actually going to be.

Save the Children showed us some upsetting sights in relation to child poverty and the use of children to mine for diamonds. Children as young as six were being asked to scrabble down holes in the ground no bigger than a dustbin lid. But as we were travelling around the desert seeing these awful sights we had no idea that an even worse tragedy was unfolding miles away. When word eventually came through that planes had hit the Twin Towers, it was worrying to be away from the children at a time of such uncertainty. We both felt very isolated with no chance to actually see the images coming from New York or get back home to our family, as all flights had been suspended.

One of the interesting aspects of the trips abroad was the chance to really get to know what other MPs were like. When I was told that Michael Howard would be a fellow delegate on a visit to Indonesia I have to confess my heart sank. In fact he was charming and enormous fun, and we had a perfectly normal conversation during downtime sat by the pool in our Jakarta hotel. The city itself was a hellhole with the worst traffic jams I'd ever seen. The daily five-mile ride to the conference centre took up to an hour. So when we received death threats after one of our delegation made some controversial remarks about human rights, I was delighted that we were immediately given a police escort which cut through the steaming jams.

One of the traditions of foreign visits is the need to pay a courtesy call on a politician that shares your political views. In my case liberals are normally easy to find, although the term means different things in some countries. Liberals in Germany are often to the right of Attila the Hun, even a bit too much for my liking.

When I visited Australia finding a real liberal was not that easy. John Howard's Liberal Party were busy turning away Indonesian boat people and I thought their Foreign Secretary, Alex Downer, was being a bit over-sensitive when he complained that I had sat in his favourite chair in his office and made me move seats at our meeting. So that left trying to hold a meeting with the almost non-existent Australian Democrats party.

The then leader, Andrew Bartlett, had a fetish for the colour purple and we'd been warned that his office was more in keeping with some hair salon than the leader of a political party. Sure enough he welcomed us in a loud purple shirt and was surrounded by purple nick-nacks – I think even the party's logo was purple.

I hated Canberra – the place was full of politicians, roads and roundabouts, and Parliament House was built underground into a hill, just like the Teletubbies house, but with a glass ceiling. Sydney, however, was wonderful and I rate the harbour area in my top three places in the world. We were taken to the state of Victoria parliament to watch a debate which turned out to be a rather riotous affair. The Speaker lost control at one point and decided to expel a member. State laws say that a member is allowed to appeal against this to the rest of the chamber and gets a few minutes to make his case. It's as if the referee gives you a red card and you can appeal to the rest of the players. In this case the British delegation of MPs watching from the public gallery didn't know what to do when the Aussie politician turned and looked up to us and said: 'Should I stay or should I go, guys – what do you think, thumbs up or down?' It was a bizarre experience, but nothing compared to the way politicians behaved in Brazil.

I'd been invited to attend a conference in Rio as part of a trans-Atlantic group that attempted to pick up-and-coming politicians and bring them together. Douglas Alexander was also invited and as events have turned out his career, unlike mine, was certainly worth investing in! Belinda joined me on the visit and whilst I spent my day debating post-9/11 international affairs, she had a series of massages on Ipanema beach from Brazilian hunks. Anyway one night we got ourselves in with some of the local MPs, an American senator and some embassy staff for a night to remember. God knows how late it was, but the Rio party spirit was alive even on the diplomatic circuit.

Drinking for your country can be a hazard but is a way of forging links in some countries. The worst or best, depending on how you look at it, are the Russians. I don't think my liver has yet completely recovered from three nights in the bizarre city of Kaliningrad. Hidden on the map and miles away from mainland Russia this little bit of land remains as a strategic link to the Baltic. It's a weird combination of old run-down Communist buildings with the most amazing hi-tech nightclubs you've ever seen. A mixture of fast Russian disco music and endless streams of vodka until five in the morning left me struggling to take in the delights of visiting the Russian fleet the next day. My heart sank on the second night when the hosts asked how many bottles we wanted with supper – vodka, that is, not wine.

Screwing Up

My favourite place in the whole world is, however, Manhattan. Every time I visit the hairs stand up on my arms as the yellow taxi heads across Brooklyn Bridge and *that* skyline comes into view. It radiates excitement, smells of adventure and I never want to leave. In 2007 I spent a wonderful three weeks in the States lecturing on the UK's special relationship with America. I lectured at Duke University in North Carolina and at Austin, Texas and combined this with visits to Los Angeles and San Francisco, but it was the few days in New York that made me realise that if I ever had the chance to work abroad, a nice apartment off Central Park would be my dream location!

Not all trips away from Westminster are fun. Ask a politician what they dread most and I guarantee the more normal ones will put the party conference at the top of any list. If they enjoy it then mark them down as bonkers. Take a mix of seaside resorts, party activists and wall-to-wall speeches and you begin to get close to the hell that occurs each year in September and October. My heart used to sink when it was Blackpool. That meant rain, rude taxi drivers, nowhere decent to eat or stay and endless trudging from venue to venue past arcades surrounded by girls in skirts no bigger than a belt. It was bloody miserable.

Let me paint the picture. The idea of Conference is to pack in as many fringe meetings and media interviews as you can in a five-day period. A fringe is a lunchtime or evening meeting with three or four speakers in front of a room of party activists who have often only turned up to get free sandwiches and escape from the rain. The delegates will do one fringe per lunchtime but we poor MPs are expected to hit at least three. In my last year as home affairs spokesman I was in such demand that I did six fringes a day, about the same number of live media interviews, a conference speech and a round of shaking hands at receptions.

It's a shattering experience. Everywhere you go party members come up and offer a word of advice or criticism or request a visit to their constituency. Then round the next corner a journalist wants a quick gossip, then a researcher needs to talk through a speech, then a lobby group wants a word, then a photo, or your signature on a manifesto or dinner with the press. It's the most intense experience and although your ego is flattered, every second is exhausting. My voice actually went one year and by the last night I was virtually miming my speech – but here's the silly thing. With such a schedule you'd think that you'd be in bed by ten – but that's where I used to go wrong. Exhausted, I would head to my room, shower, put on some jeans and hit the conference bar.

Now the Lib Dems may be the third party of politics but if elections were decided on bar takings we would be heading for a landslide. Each year from Blackpool, Bournemouth to Brighton the main conference hotel would under-estimate the amount of late-night drinking the party members would get through. The tradition is that, late at night, activists, MPs and sometimes party leaders chat at the bar. Paddy Ashdown would regularly pitch up, hiding a cigarette behind his back from his wife. I was awful, often staying up till four or five and then having to do the *Today* programme at seven. I remember one year having to keep in close proximity to a hotel litter bin in case I threw up on air. The problem is that after such a horrid and exhausting day you just need to unwind and then when you hit the bar it's impossible to leave. You get into long chats with fellow MPs in a drunken way that's refreshing. Then the lobby correspondents with their big expense accounts chuck drinks at you. After a few years you become matey with them and at two in the morning everybody is gossiping like mad. They must love the information they get. I remember one year a group of us had about five lobby hacks back to a room in the hotel. A member of the House of Lords was picking up the tab and more and more food and drink was ordered up. I am not sure what was going on but a couple of major news correspondents managed to break off the loo seat, which eventually ended up round somebody's head. It was outrageous behaviour – and the next day I was giving interviews to them as if nothing had happened.

I hardly ever saw anyone take drugs at conference. Hard though it is to believe, I've never taken any drugs myself, not even a drag of a joint. I have plenty of other sins but the whole drug thing scares me. It's not so much a moral thing – just a fear of what they may do to me. It goes back a long way. Some of my schoolmates indulged and one in particular seemed to have everything under the sun at his house. At times I felt a bit left out as they kept concocting different ways to get high. They were even growing the stuff: my mate's mother had no idea what she was watering on top of the fridge but it certainly was not the type of thing to put into the local WI show. I am also very aware of the need to avoid drinking too much. It's an occupational hazard but one I've kept under control over the years.

The dangerous mix at Conference of people who worked and got drunk together led to plenty of room-hopping in the early hours. The journalists, MPs and exhibition stand organisers were often exchanging more than stories, which would create a few awkward breakfast meetings the next day. I was falling into this weird world. Long hours, late-night drinking, journalists and gossip. I was starting to become part of 'The Establishment' – the kind of egotistic MP I'd promised not be. Things were heading in the wrong direction and the warning signs were starting to stare me in the face, if only I'd been watching.

4

Kennedy buffer zone

My first years in Parliament were dominated by the leadership of Paddy Ashdown and stormy parliamentary party meetings as he flirted closer and closer with the idea of a pact under Tony Blair. I was an Ashdown loyalist but at the time had little idea just how far his so-called 'project' was going with Labour.

Paddy liked to spring things on his parliamentary colleagues and this created a number of showdowns at our meetings. He also had a slight habit of over-stating the importance of each issue, starting any debate with a warning to colleagues that this was the most important decision they were likely to take – a warning he would repeat on a different subject a few weeks later. Shortly after the 1997 election Ashdown was involved in secret discussions with Blair over a form of merger between their two parties which was known as the 'Full Monty'; the plans were kept hidden from all but a few colleagues. We knew that before the election there had been plans within the 'project' to form a post-election arrangement under a Joint Cabinet Committee (JCC). With Labour's thumping majority, no coalition was necessary, but Ashdown was still determined to push ahead. This outraged colleagues, who felt he was going too far.

His diaries during this year show that the JCC was just the tip of the iceberg and the real agenda was not just electoral reform, but moves towards a merger with Labour. I interviewed David Steel about this period as part of my 2007 book on coalitions. Steel was surprised at just how far Ashdown was prepared to go, telling me: 'I thought I was a bit out in front of the party, but he was miles out in front.' For my part, I never had a problem with him challenging the party. After all, his brilliant leadership had dragged the party from 5 per cent in the polls to its best election result in decades.

At the same time discussions on changing the voting system had been dragging on and on until it was agreed to establish an electoral reform commission to be headed by Roy Jenkins. This was to be Jenkins's last big political job. After such a distinguished career it's sad that Blair used him in what turned out to be rather a non-job, publishing a set of proposals which seemed fated to do no more than gather dust – although the issue was raised again a decade later when Gordon Brown's government faced a need to reform after the MPs' expenses scandal.

It was clear to those involved that the commission's work would take some time to complete and even if it were to get Blair's endorsement and parliamentary time there was little prospect of a new voting system at the next election. Ashdown was aware that without proportional representation he had to help protect his new clutch of MPs and win yet more. Part of the Blair discussions involved very private work on how the two parties could help in a cluster of seats where the Labour vote could make a difference to a Lib Dem victory.

By early 1998, most meetings of the Liberal parliamentary party were dominated by talk of the project. There was an obsession amongst some MPs with the subject as they wanted to know how many times Blair and Ashdown met and the details of the meetings. Ashdown was constantly on the back foot as he gave his weekly leader's report at the Wednesday night meetings. You could see the look of despair come across his face if Jackie Ballard or David Rendel, two left-leaning MPs, put their hands up to speak on the subject. Most MPs fell into one of three camps on the issue. Those pro-Ashdown and part of the inner circle were keen that the talks continued although they were not sure where they would end. Those firmly opposed, wanting an independent party, were annoyed at the secrecy and deeply mistrustful of Ashdown. A third group – by far the largest – were more interested in getting focus leaflets delivered to ensure they got re-elected and as long as Ashdown was not costing votes by talking to Blair they would watch with marginal interest. I got rather frustrated at the endless time wasted on the issue, but was firmly in the Ashdown camp, believing he was right to continue with the project. After all his leadership had delivered a large number of seats, mine included, and when I looked at those who argued for the project they were on the more sound wing of the party in my judgement. It's also important to remember that at the time Blair was unstoppable, riding high in the polls, certainly heading for a second term and not yet as worryingly illiberal as he was to become. So there was appeal in hanging onto the shirt tails of such a popular Prime Minister. However, I had no idea at the time just how grand Ashdown's true plans were.

In the end it all resulted in, well, nothing. Blair never agreed to proportional representation and Ashdown could never take his colleagues with him on plans to increase co-operation. At a very emotional parliamentary party meeting shortly into 1999 he shocked most of us by announcing his resignation.

Amidst the tears it was interesting to note who rushed out of the meeting in Committee Room 11 to hit the phones for a possible leadership contest. For my part I decided to back the pro-Ashdown candidate, the easy-going and very sensible MP for Bath, Don Foster. Along with Lembit Öpik I pushed Don's cause until it became clear that Charles Kennedy was unstoppable. With Don's full support we all jumped ship. To this day I have an old yellow 'Foster for Leadership' T-shirt which I wear in bed. Hardly a turn-on for Belinda, I admit.

When Kennedy took over as leader in 1999 I was surprised to be asked to become his PPS (parliamentary private secretary). It took me from the back benches to the heart of the party's leadership. Working with Charles was a rollercoaster existence. At his best he's one of the most intuitive politicians I know. His instincts on the big issues are spot on, he is a great communicator and wonderfully unstuffy for a politician. I was delighted to discover that he loathed long meetings and despaired at the Liberal

Democrats' obsession with party committees. To his horror he found that as leader he was actually expected to chair some of them. Charles much preferred the informal approach – a small close-knit group that he would call into his office for 'a quick gossip'. Always sitting at his desk he would kick off his shoes, plonk his feet on the table, with the rest of us slouched on sofas, and wander through an agenda. It was in this setting that decisions on the big issues of the day such as the war in Iraq really took place rather than any formal party meetings.

At one of our 'gossip sessions' shortly after he became leader we began to realise that his performance at Prime Minister's Questions (PMQ) was being affected by none other than the former Prime Minister Edward Heath. As father of the House (the Westminster title for the longest-serving MP) Heath was allowed to sit where he liked in the Commons. As a sign of his semi-detachment from the Conservatives he positioned himself next to the Tory front bench, on the bench occupied by the Liberal Democrats. This had not been a problem for Paddy Ashdown, for he preferred the slightly elevated position of the bench in the second row to deliver his questions to the Prime Minister, but Kennedy felt much more secure in the front row with his feet firmly on the floor of the House. So for the first few sessions of PMQ, Charles was snuggled up to Heath and I, as his PPS, sat on the other side of Charles.

Now at the time Heath was in his early eighties and, rather like many men of that age, was often partial to a nap or a snooze. PMQ was often the trigger for this and frankly, given that PMQ is largely a waste of time, I am somewhat sympathetic to Heath wanting to doze through it. In my view if you are going to have a power nap, those thirty minutes are probably the best time to do it, but that didn't help the Kennedy team. The image it left, especially on TV, was of Kennedy asking his question with Heath slumped next to him, eyes shut and perhaps dreaming about yachting, or conducting, but certainly showing no interest at all in what Charles was asking. The solution, after endless 'gossip meetings', was to move Kennedy one place down the bench and put me in between him and Heath. My instructions were clear: as Charles stood up I would give Heath a slight nudge in his ribs and suddenly the elder statesman would spring into life. To the outside world as he woke up he looked perfectly alert whilst my boss was asking his question. The task was known as 'being the Heath buffer zone' and I quickly performed my first important parliamentary role as Kennedy's PPS.

Sitting next to Heath was rather fun – as a boy aged eight I can remember seeing him as Prime Minister on TV and enjoying the smell of candles and hunting for batteries as the power cuts took place under his watch. Over three decades later I was privileged to sit next to him and enjoy his running commentaries on the performance of William Hague at PMQ. Heath didn't talk much; instead, he tended to let out was an occasional grumble or grunt when Hague said something he disapproved of. This would begin to form in his lower abdomen and gradually work its way through his belly, until he exhaled with a kind of groaning sound. On one occasion the groaning sound was particularly audible and clear – Hague had been asking one of his more outrageous questions on the European Union and Heath immediately turned round and said: 'What a vulgar little man.' I think he'd rather approve of Hague these days as, rather like a fresh wine, he has become a better politician with age.

On most occasions my main focus was making sure that I was supportive to Charles asking his questions. It is actually a nightmare preparing for PMQ, particularly if you are the leader of the third party. Hours would be spent considering what subject to 'go on'. Meetings would start on Monday and discussions would continue until the Wednesday morning, whereupon about four people would sit in Charles's office to role play the proposed questions. It became a badge of honour to be involved in this discussion and parliamentary colleagues would regularly submit suggestions which mostly, frankly, were off the mark. In particular, Bob Russell, our enthusiastic and popular MP for Colchester, would ask each week without fail if we could submit a question on Boy Scouts!

On every occasion we would have to second-guess what the subject of the day would be, but more particularly, given that Charles would come after the leader of the Conservative Party, we knew that any killer question we had might become a waste of time if the Tory leader had chosen to go on a similar subject. We always took in a back-up question just in case. On most occasions the back-up system worked, but there was one awful Wednesday when William Hague chose to cover a couple of subjects on his first wave of questions. Charles and I glanced at each other relatively calmly when he asked our first question, but a look of panic came over our faces the minute those dulcet Yorkshire tones started to form what had been our back-up question. With hardly seconds to spare before the Speaker was due to call Charles next, I muttered to him: 'What the hell are you going to ask now?' Just as he got to his feet he turned to me and in his broad Scottish accent said: 'Ah, Mark, I have absolutely no idea, but you know this is better than having a real job,' and then went on to ask a brilliant question. Those were occasions when Charles was a total pleasure to work with.

The sociable side of Charles attracted an interesting bunch of celebrities that would happily spend an evening with the leader of the third party and in some cases offer support to the cause. The Kennedy team arranged a number of 'at homes' in Charles's flat near Victoria. On one occasion the combination of David Frost, Bob Geldof and Joanna Lumley, all together in his kitchen, made for an odd evening and although I was a bit star struck next to Patsy from *Ab Fab*, this event, like the others, was good fun. I always drank far too much but I can just about remember long rambling conversations with the likes of George Melly and, bizarrely, making a complete fool of myself with inappropriate *Some Mothers Do 'Ave 'Em* jokes with the long suffering star of that show, Michele Dotrice.

Obviously it was not all plain sailing and others have recorded elsewhere Charles's difficulties with drink. Charles himself acknowledged this when he resigned as party leader and it is certainly not my intention to dwell on the subject. I have no wish to hurt or harm Charles as he was very loyal to me and gave me wonderful opportunities in the party. However, it was at times a very stressful situation and I just can't write an honest account of my time at Westminster without recalling a couple of examples of the type of pressure we were under at the time.

Before I became Charles's PPS I was aware of the rumours about his drinking, but had no personal experience of it myself. His leadership campaign in 1999 was the first moment that many of the 1997 intake of

MPs were made aware of the problem. The candidates standing against Charles often made cryptic references to it.

For the most part during his leadership Charles was in fact on top of his game and in my judgement a superb politician. He had a great affinity with the British public and an ability to see the wood for the trees on major issues, but when the off days happened it was tough on all those in his close team. If we had not liked, or admired, him so much then it would have been easy to tell him to sort the drinking out or quit, but very few had the heart or stomach to take on the issue. In all my time as his PPS, or as party chairman, I never once raised the question of his drinking with him. Although we were politically close, and out of all the MPs I had the most access to him, I would not describe our relationship as the kind of friendship that can develop between work colleagues and as such I found it painful to have a heart-to-heart with him; for his part he was incredibly private and shy on personal matters. The brunt of the tough-love conversations fell to his closest advisor, Anna Werrin, who on several occasions threatened to leave, and this would then result in a period of good weeks.

Getting Charles to make it to big events was often a problem. Increasingly he would leave it very late to arrive at the office for PMQ. The team liked to prepare him as early as possible, but on more than one occasion it was a white-knuckle ride to see if he would make it in time. Various aides would be sent to get him ready. Sometimes I would be sitting on the bench watching the Commons clock getting closer to twelve with an empty space next to me as I tried to calm down anxious colleagues.

You were never 100 per cent sure Charles would turn up until you actually had him in your sights, but even that was no guarantee he would see something through. Once I'd been due to accompany him on a foreign trip. I was at Heathrow airport, about to walk through Departures, when word came through that Charles had disappeared. The trip never went ahead.

One of the worst times with Charles coincided with a spring party conference in Southport. Cold, windy and full of girls with skimpy skirts, the whole weekend is ingrained on my memory. Rumours were flying around amongst MPs and the journalists that Charles was in a bad way. He was, and I was deeply concerned for his health. He had lost weight, looked weak and was clearly very wobbly. During one of the rehearsals for his speech we cleared the auditorium of all but the group closest to him and went through the latest version, clutching fish and chips. Much to my horror Charles asked me to go on stage and deliver part of the speech. By the time he was to deliver the speech on Sunday morning I felt it was touch and go whether he could do it himself. When he did take to the stage he looked pale, sounded hoarse and under the stage lights needed to wipe sweat from his face. However, by the end we all felt it had gone OK and we had got away without too much damage. The media pack saw it differently. The next day's press was a nightmare, the worst I had known – all carrying pictures of Charles looking like death warmed up. The knives were really out now and I feared he might not last long in the job.

Charles is not the only memorable figure I've known around Westminster. Lembit Öpik is one of the more colourful in our party and I am pleased to call him a friend. Annoyingly full of energy, he is always up to something: paragliding, picking up weather girls and Cheeky Girls, running an airline, or running for some kind of office; he is brilliantly mad. Although not all of my colleagues are fans he has shown enormous loyalty, first to Charles and also towards me during my nightmare months. His sleeping habits are perhaps the most annoying thing about him – not his choice of women, but rather his timekeeping. I don't think he actually sleeps at all! I have been a fair few times at late-night clubs and pubs around Soho and Westminster playing chess with him, only to hear him on the radio the next day as if the word 'hangover' did not exist.

He brought Gaby, his ex-Cheeky Girlfriend, down for a weekend in Winchester and it was then that I realised just how much of a celeb he'd become. My two daughters were delighted to have a Cheeky Girl in the house and laid on their own *X Factor*-style dance routine to impress her. The next day I agreed to drive Lembit and Gaby to Popham airport so he could fly on to Wales. As we walked across this small rural airstrip the local flying enthusiasts turned their attention from the air towards Lembit and Gaby. They actually formed a small guard of honour, clapped and wondered who the hell I was as I followed along carrying their luggage. That's the power of *All Star Mr and Mrs* over *Newsnight*!

I am told by those who went to public school that the House of Commons is a bit like an Eton for grown-ups. The place is stuffy, smelly and full of stupid traditions. There is a clubby atmosphere that I have never felt comfortable with. It is very male dominated and exclusive. The eating and drinking arrangements sum the place up.

The Tea Room is perhaps the most famous. The media loves to talk about potential leadership candidates needing to work the Tea Room. It is long and narrow, furnished with tables and comfy chairs. The Labour MPs sit at one end, Tories at the other and one table is set aside for the Lib Dems. In the middle there is a selection of sandwiches, hot drinks and sticky buns. Each table is piled high with newspapers and the room is filled with the low tones of gossip. When I first turned up as a newly elected MP, I had no idea about the segregation rules and plonked myself down at the end of one of the Conservative tables. I soon sensed something was wrong when John Redwood sat next to me looking rather bemused to see me. It was all rather terrifying. I now sit on the correct table, but close enough to listen to the Tories gossiping. The Tea Room is better than any opinion poll: you can really sense and hear the concerns within each party.

The Tea Room serves as the MPs' café or bistro but for a full meal we have the Members' Dining Room. You can take guests there for lunch, but when night falls this large hall becomes one of London's most exclusive private restaurants. 'Members Only' means just that, only members of the House of Commons or House of Lords who used to be MPs are allowed in. Again there is segregation. There are about twelve tables with the Tories at one end, Labour at the other and, you've guessed it, the Lib Dems and Nationalists left to fight it out over two tables in the centre of the room. The menu is full of real schoolboy stuff – mushy peas, fish and chips and spotted dick. Jamie Oliver would have a field day here. I guess I hated and loved it at the same time. Some nights when you are stuck waiting for votes till 10 p.m. it is a life saver to have the company of colleagues. I would often agree to share a bottle of wine and tuck into three courses and a good gossip. I never knew who would be at the table, but if Ming Campbell, Paddy

Ashdown or Don Foster were around a good evening was guaranteed. MPs generally share stories about what they have been up to, their funny constituents and tips on how to save and use the various expenses and allowances. Meals are often interrupted with votes – it is a strange scene. Imagine a restaurant where suddenly every guest gets up and walks out! Nothing is more annoying than your fish pie arriving nice and hot and then the division bell goes and you return ten minutes later to a cold plate. Occasionally the wonderful waiters take half-eaten meals back to the kitchen to keep warm. It is a dangerous world: you can end up eating and drinking far too much in a place where your only company is fellow MPs.

The late-night atmosphere at Westminster is at its best or worst, depending on your view, during the month leading up to the summer recess. As the sun sets on the terrace overlooking the Thames, honourable members spill out from the Strangers' Bar carrying trays of Pimm's and champagne for teams of researchers or party colleagues. As we wait for the ten o'clock division the balmy summer evening is fuelled by cheap alcohol, creating a gossipy atmosphere.

Inevitably late drinking and late working combined lead to affairs and indiscretions. I have never been in the bars enough to know about all the affairs taking place, but when I do walk into the Strangers' Bar there are a set number of MPs I can bet on seeing; the only real variation is which young researcher they will be flirting with that night. I am told that some colleagues will even spot somebody in the public gallery during the debates and seek them out with the offer of a private tour and drink later. It may come as no surprise that those chosen tend to be young and female. I don't for a moment judge colleagues, as I am in no position, but it does amaze me that this goes on under the nose of so many without it ever becoming public knowledge. Perhaps that's because so many of the lobby correspondents are often up to no good themselves. I remember gossiping with an ITV reporter about a female Labour MP I'd heard was having an affair. 'Yes,' he said. 'It's with me!' Whoops! He went on to say how sweet it was that I had no idea!

In the end my life became so busy that the evenings ended up packed with events, speeches and meetings that never allowed the luxury of an hour for supper. I have not been to the Members' Dining Room since my scandal as it's a reminder of my old life which had become too focused on the clubby atmosphere I had never really felt at home in.

The Jurassic Park life is not limited to eating. The very business of politics takes on a world of its own. We call ourselves 'Honourable Members' and in debates we name each other after our constituency. I became Winchester, not Mark Oaten. When I arrived I dreaded the moment in a debate when I wanted to refer to what another MP had said as I had no idea what constituency they represented. Thankfully a 'major' modernisation has now allowed the big green monitors to add on the name of a member's constituency when they speak. Speaking in the chamber is a truly awful experience because of these rules. You can't just speak your mind and talk as if in a public meeting or to your mates, instead you have to watch your language. You cannot address another Member directly, but have to speak via the Speaker. You cannot call the House of Lords by its name; in our world it's called 'the other place'. I've never felt comfortable speaking in the chamber. For the Lib Dem spokesman it is made worse by the position you have to speak from. If you are the minister or the Tory shadow there is a wonderfully protective dispatch box bang in front of you which is ideal for notes, a glass of water and to lean on. As a poor old Lib Dem you have nothing but the prospect of looking at Dennis Skinner as you shuffle around with your notes flapping about in front of you.

The Chamber itself is remarkably small. A strong aroma of stale whisky and rotting mice hit me when I arrived and I found it terrifying to sit on the green benches as I worried about breaking rules and procedures with my every movement. Walking in and out involves careful steps to a white line and then nodding to the Speaker; the whole place is full of hazards likely to trip you up. The actual benches themselves might be real leather but are bloody uncomfortable when you are stuck, your bum gradually numbing, during a five-hour debate. Taking a break is frowned on and might risk the Speaker dropping you from the little list of speakers he keeps to the left of his chair.

The longest I think I've been stuck in there was back in January 2000, when for some reason we were voting throughout the night on some

Northern Ireland issues. These always drag on and I happened to be covering for our spokesman. At one point, around 4.30 a.m., when hardly anybody was listening to some dull rant from an Ulster Unionist a, mouse decided it was safe enough to come out. It ran around, crossed the famous red lines, hit my shoe and woke us all up. Of course the press the next day upgraded it to a rat in the chamber!

I have often felt as though I am working in a museum. As the tourists are given official tours you can even hear the guides pointing you out like an exhibit – 'That's Mark Oaten, he won his seat by two votes, and more recently he had a famous scandal.' However, not every part of Westminster is stuffy and old; Portcullis House has the touch of a modern shopping mall with trees that drop leaves and low-level fountains that never seem to work. It's surrounded with restaurants and European-style coffee bars. The place is full of twenty-something researchers rushing around between their cappuccinos or strutting self-importantly, wide eyed and full of enthusiasm, en route in a few years' time to a nice little earner with a public affairs consultancy. Older and with even more self-grandeur the MPs pass from meeting to meeting as they listen to pressure groups make their case over coffee. Look around at any given time and you can see the glazed look of a politician being lobbied for the umpteenth time that day. I try to keep each meeting to 40 minutes. If someone can't explain themselves in that time, then tough. Many of the public affairs people get paid more than me so they should be able to think and account for their clients quicker than me.

Amongst the 644 MPs there is now a vast spread of age and background and there are more women than ever before. Whilst there are numerous political differences there are also common traits. I've yet to find an MP without an enormous ego; many of us hide it well, but to have stood for public office in the first place demonstrates vanity, the need to be loved and a certain thickness of skin.

Within a few months of being called 'Sir' by House of Commons staff and with those MP initials suddenly opening doors, it's hardly a surprise that we become far too self-important for our own good. We hunt out our press cuttings, love being asked for an autograph and cannot resist the one-upmanship of showing off to colleagues. Don't get me wrong, most of my colleagues are great fun, decent, nice and totally committed to what they do for the right reasons, but still hidden in there is this strange political curse. The worst are some of the Labour backbenchers. They make the dullest long-winded speeches in debates, waiting for hours to be called at 8.35 p.m. on a Tuesday night and deliver twenty minutes of garbage. Honestly! As if anyone gives a damn at that time of night.

Some of the old Tories, the so-called 'Knights of the Shires', are so crusty they could snap. However, sometimes appearances can be deceptive. Take Sir Patrick Cormack, the longest-serving MP bar one. He is very serious and proper in the chamber and a real Commons man. I got to know him well when I was asked to become one of the editors of the *House Magazine* – MPs' in-house reading. Patrick was the main editor and we met every Tuesday morning in his office. I soon realised this grand old Tory had wonderful kindness and humour. He has always been utterly decent and along with another knight, Sir George Young, would have made an excellent Speaker in the Commons.

Throughout my time at the *House Magazine* I was able to work alongside some wonderful colleagues: Austin Mitchell, Ruth Kelly, Gisela Stuart and Michael Gove. The Tuesday morning meetings became one of the highlights of the week as we gossiped, told each other what was really going on, all in the confidence that there never had been or would be a leak. I deeply regretted that one of the consequences of my scandal was that the owners of the magazine sacked me within days.

There are of course differences between the parties with traditions built up over years. You're more likely to find an ex-trade union leader or academic in New Labour. The Tories have plenty of lawyers and businessmen whilst the Lib Dems have often come from a public sector and local government background. OK, that's an over-simplification and one of the consequences of first New Labour and now Cameron's softer Conservatives is a blurring of these stereotypes. But around Westminster we still have our own differences.

Each of the political parties has its own backbenchers' group. The Conservatives' is known as the 1922 Committee and they meet at the same time as the Liberal Democrats gather, just a few rooms away from each other every Wednesday afternoon on the committee corridor. For two years I chaired our meetings, but for most of my ten years I've sat at the back watching the clock to see when I could get away. We very rarely discuss matters of great importance, instead often dwelling for hours on presentations, on how to win elections or claim expenses. Lembit Öpik and I often sit together moaning about the waste of our time on such issues of detail.

The grass is always greener on the other side and I imagined the Conservatives' meetings full of plans to get into government, although for much of the last decade they faced endless crises and the press pack gathered outside their committee room as leadership elections took place. In the end that particular problem was to move a few rooms down the corridor and it was to be my party surrounded by journalists as we lurched into our own crisis.

5

Arsenic for Paxman and Humphrys in the nude

As we headed towards the 2001 election I was being asked to do more and more media work for the party and was starting to get to know some of the journalists and political pundits who dominate Westminster.

As an aspiring MP you spend hours watching and listening to the likes of Paxman, Humphrys and Dimbleby – now all of a sudden I found myself in the hot seat becoming one of the regulars on *Newsnight*, *Today* and *Question Time*. It felt unreal at times: hang on, I'm just a boy from Watford after all, but these people are icons – or so I thought!

When people ask me about the job, the first question is often: have you met the Queen? (Yes I have: she was remarkably small and very pleasant.) That is often followed by: what's Jeremy Paxman really like?

Well, two episodes spring to mind. For some inexplicable reason I had been put up to represent the party on a *Newsnight* Budget special programme. Now I have as much hope of understanding the Budget as I have of becoming a rocket scientist – but nevertheless I found myself doing the usual route in the BBC car at 9.45 p.m. heading for Television Centre.

Screwing Up

The drill is much the same every time: the party press office pages you around six, just when you are praying for an early evening, and tells you *Newsnight* has put a bid in for you. You get to the green room at 10.15 p.m., a small pokey affair with coffee and a television, with a make-up room next door. Make-up by this time is badly needed: I am hardly Nixon, but my stubble is showing and my eyes are baggy. When you sit down and the make-up lady starts to dab at you, you immediately feel sleepy as it is often the first chance you have had to sit down and stop all day. Paxman bounces in at this point, saying hi, and the next time you meet is in the studio.

On this particular occasion I was involved in a 'disco', an annoying media term that means studio discussion, and not that Oliver Letwin, Dawn Primarolo and I were going to boogie down to the sounds of DJ Paxo. The media world is full of this jargon, which you soon get to learn. Other phrases you come to terms with in the media world include 'eng', 'pre-rec', 'noddy', 'down the line' and 'as live' – all variations on the type of interview you might be giving.

Anyway, in the studio the *Newsnight* music fades away and Paxman proceeds to grill the Chief Secretary to the Treasury and Conservative shadow Chancellor on spending commitments and taxation. Eventually, almost as an afterthought, the chair swivels round and he faces me and asks: 'Now, Mr Oaten, how much will your party's commitment be to cod liver oil costs?'

What the hell is that about? It's not in my briefing papers – what shall I say? 'Well, Jeremy, the party is very committed to health and preventative care.'

Paxman's not letting go. 'Yes, but is it costed and how much for?'

Oh, for God's sake! Ask me about education, or tax, or anything, I've just got no idea on this one. 'Well, healthcare costs so much that we think that keeping people better will save money in the long run.' Oh dear, that was a terrible answer – he's going to kill me off now.

He's starting to enjoy himself. 'So you really have no idea, Mr Oaten, it's not costed. It could be millions – how are you going to pay for it?'

OK, this is awful but I am fighting back now. 'Jeremy, frankly I suggest you take some, it might do you some good!' Oh no, ground swallow me up! Look at that expression. I can even sense the other guests beginning to feel pity for me. Fifty seconds of questions that felt like an hour and I'd never even heard of the damn policy.

The next day I found out that our former children's spokesman, Dr Jenny Tonge, had vaguely suggested that free cod liver oil for all would be in the nation's interest. I got a fair bit of ribbing from colleagues, a few even miming a spoon of medicine going into the mouth from the other side of the chamber. Anyway, the story has a happy ending. I was determined to show Paxman that I could take a joke and that weekend found myself in the local Winchester branch of Holland & Barrett in search of cod liver oil. I posted a small bottle to the *Newsnight* offices and a week later I got a note back:

Dear Mark
Thank you so much for the bottle of cod liver oil. General consensus in the office is best not to open as likely to be arsenic.

P.S. What's the party line on evening primrose oil?

A few weeks later I was back in the studio on a more comfortable subject, police reforms, but just as the music faded, Paxman muttered to me: 'Now I am going to ask you about cod liver oil again!' I guess it would have been worse to make a blunder and commit the party to some new tax proposals, or even to forget what our VAT policy was. I hated questions on finance, as I have an enormous struggle with numbers – I failed my O-level maths three times and never even bothered to collect my result when I took it for a fourth time a year after I had left school. Twenty years later I was invited back to the same school to address the pupils at a special assembly. I mentioned my failure to pass maths and my unknown final result. Remarkably by the end of the speech the head teacher was able to announce that during my talk he had delved into the archives and found my exam result. With some drama building up in the hall he unveiled the piece of paper and announced to everybody that yes, it was another failure. That was no surprise; what was remarkable, however, was the school filing system!

Screwing Up

Away from the *Newsnight* studio I had another public encounter with Paxman. I had agreed to take part in a celebrity version of *University Challenge*. After an early start and a drive to Manchester I found myself on the politics team, facing a team from the media including Nick Robinson and Bridget Kendall, who seemed much better qualified than we did. In the studio before the recording started we were asked to test whether our buzzers worked – I guess I was a little bit over-enthusiastic and kept hitting mine as hard as I could. Paxman turned to the audience and said: 'I doubt we will hear much from Mr Oaten's buzzer when the real programme starts.' He was right. I was frozen. I was not brave enough to hit the buzzer when I knew the answer and afraid to take what could be a stupid guess on other questions. It's a lot easier watching at home.

As a child I remember lying in front of the fire watching Bamber Gascoigne ask the questions and listening to my parents pitching their wits against each other. They made a great team. My father as a classicist and my mother's knowledge of the arts seemed to regularly put the floppy-haired students, with their daft teddy bear mascots, in their place. It was one of the few times my parents actually seemed to enjoy each other's company – even though it was based on a high element of one-upmanship. Years later I think my mum was rather pleased that my two-vote election win was one of the questions on the programme. She certainly got that one right.

One of the downsides of 24-hour media is that they want you for twenty-four hours. It often means early starts on breakfast TV or the *Today* programme. I hated early mornings and would do anything to try to dodge a *Today* bid by telling the party press office that perhaps the story we had was not very strong, or that I was not really clear what the party line should be and maybe it would be better in these circumstances to avoid giving an interview.

In the end I could not keep saying no and decided to install my own ISDN line and mini-studio at home. It changed my life. The 7.20 a.m. slot on the *Today* programme no longer involved the very early start and trip to the studio. Instead I would literally crawl out of bed, switch on the unit and go on air. Now I know this is not a pretty image for you, but on some occasions I would sit in my boxer shorts, or in various forms of undress, covered in shaving foam as I discussed the merits of terrorism legislation.

On the *Today* programme, when people asked me 'how do you deal with John Humphrys', I would say 'buck naked, that's how'! It wasn't all plain sailing, as dogs, cats and children would often barge in, but I managed to master the technique of talking very calmly on air, whilst moving one leg up to block the door, or scribbling a note to the children telling them to shut up. Who said men can't multitask!

Nakedness and the *Today* programme seemed to go together. I was doing a 'disco' with David Davis and Jim Naughtie from my flat in south London. At the time I had a flatmate in his twenties, a Westminster researcher, who seemed to have a string of girlfriends sleeping over. This particular morning I was in the kitchen doing an interview when his latest conquest casually walked in, completely naked, took a glass, filled it with water from the tap, smiled at me and walked out. It took all of my concentration to discuss identity cards without slipping up and declaring that they would not stop any more boobs in London.

The worst experience of all is appearing on *Question Time* – I have done thirteen in my life as an MP and every one has been nerve-racking. Whenever I hear that rather annoying signature tune my stomach churns. The BBC's obsession with wanting to look 'non-London-centric' means you end up travelling to all sorts of locations throughout the UK. Sometimes that's alright. One show was filmed at the Eden Project, and when it was lit up it looked something like you might find in a James Bond movie set with David Dimbleby doing his best to look like Blofeld minus the cat.

Normally the programme takes place in a cold school building with a local parent/teachers' association providing curled-up sandwiches for the panel to force down their increasingly dry throats. Personally, I always need a couple of glasses of wine before I go on and I remember once in Doncaster there wasn't a drop in sight until after the show. Getting the alcohol level right is tricky: too little and you are extremely nervous, too much perhaps a bit cocky. Two glasses and a sandwich seem to do the trick for me, but I have seen some first-timers come on and absolutely crash after they've had too many drinks in the green room only to regret it midway through the programme.

People often think that the panel gets to see the questions in advance; well, they don't, although frankly it is not that tricky to figure out what is going to be in the news each week. However, it is demanding to provide a decent response in just a minute and what you actually dread is Dimbleby, and this goes for his brother too, turning to you first. I have never frozen, but must confess to a little cheating on one occasion – it is hardly a *Who Wants to be a Millionaire* coughing moment, but I was sitting next to David Dimbleby and was able to quickly glance down and see what the second question was ahead of time. However, on nearly every other programme I have done I have been stuck right at the far end of the table in a position whereby the ugly lump on the side of my neck has pride of place on camera. Almost like a sixth panellist in fact. You can imagine Dimbleby turning to the lump and asking what it thinks of party policy on wind farms or alternative fuels.

In fact the lump has been with me for about ten years. It's a cyst and Belinda keeps saying she will hang decorations on it if it's not removed by next Christmas – or put another way, if you're old enough to remember *Spitting Image*, my cyst is a bit like David Steel's puppet coming out of David Owen's neck. I am just too much of a wimp to have it cut out. Dr Jenny Tonge, a former fellow MP, now in the House of Lords, said she could do it on the green Commons benches with a sharp knife in the time it took to sit and watch Prime Minister's Questions. People even used to email me and ask about the lump after a TV programme.

I have always found the two Dimbleby brothers a pleasure to work with, a bit grand and scary on the first occasion, but when you become a regular they are friendly and enjoyable company. My *Any Questions* experience has twice involved being chaired by the late Nick Clarke, who was also to interview me many times for *The World at One*. We had supper on a couple of occasions at party conference and he was one of nicest people you could imagine, charming, self-deprecating and very funny. His death was a real loss to broadcasting.

The rounds of lunches and suppers seem to grow as you become better known to the journalists. I hate long lunches and suppers and get fidgety quite quickly. Nevertheless I got to know Nick Robinson, Tom Bradby and Peter Riddell well as a result of them. Without exception I found them all thoroughly good fun and decent individuals. Whilst the whole lobby as a pack is awful, individually they are a delight to work with. Tom, in particular, is a fascinating character, from royal correspondent to the political chief at ITV; he is one of their rising stars – the Ant or Dec of current affairs. In fact you could really hate him: good looks, lovely family, great job and even a best-selling author as well.

Although every media interview has the potential to go badly wrong, the good news is that on the whole you're often the only person to notice a mistake. You soon realise that most listeners or viewers are not actually hanging on to your every word and often don't know what you're banging on about. Your voice, or face, is background to their busy morning. Constituents will often say they heard you on the radio, make a kind remark, then go on to say they've no idea what you were talking about. That's the real world. The unreal world of politics means we get cuttings and transcripts giving us an over-inflated view that what we say matters. Some days the daily cuttings would show I was mentioned in ten national newspapers. My ego was well and truly stroked and I thought I'd earned my pay – until I remembered I was the only person that gets a summary of all ten clips. If you're lucky a voter will have bought a paper that day and if you're even luckier may have turned to see the article on ID cards on page 5 and perhaps made it to the paragraphs with your quote. The daily cutting service boosts our egos but is a poor indicator of what the world beyond Westminster really hears.

It can be enormously frustrating to spend a day jumping in and out of TV and radio studios, writing articles and briefing journalists to be then told the next day by a taxi driver that they've no idea what the party position is on *x* or *y*. Worse still are the angry emails from party members asking why you're not doing more to publicise our position on ASBOs or prison over-crowding. They may have been in the garden during *The World at One* and watching *Emmerdale* when you were on *Channel 4 News*. It's a lottery and you only ever get known, or heard, when the sheer volume of coverage reaches a tipping point. I reckon it took about two years of regular coverage before my name got anywhere near some national recognition and even then probably only 2 or 3 per cent of the public knew who I was. In reality it took a scandal to achieve a high level of recognition and I don't recommend that as a route for aspiring Lib Dems. For most of us we are just about a household name in our own household. My favourite and most often used way of explaining the mismatch between our ego and the reality is the apocryphal story of the MP who visits a nursing home. He is a bit put out when one old lady seems less than interested in shaking his hand so he pompously declares: 'Do you know who I am?' The old lady responds 'No, love, but if you ask Matron she will tell you.'

There is, however, one group that does listen to and read what you say. Colleagues and enemies alike will often pore over your words hoping to catch you out, or see what the latest policy line is. If I wanted to know what our Treasury team were saying on inheritance tax the press clippings were as good a guide as anything else. There's also the sad fact that often the only people watching *Newsnight* or the Sunday political programmes are the politicians themselves.

I soon became aware that commenting on your opponents in the privacy of a radio booth is one thing, but then you have to look them in the eye hours later in the corridors around Westminster. I am not by nature a parliamentary bruiser and hate making an issue personal. In all my time as a spokesman I've avoided calling for resignations, bar one occasion, which I still remember and regret. I was party chairman at the time and Keith Vaz, a minister for Europe, was caught in some controversy concerning two businessmen, the Hinduja brothers. Charles Kennedy's office wanted us to get in the news agenda and we'd been promised a good slot on *The World at One* if we'd go so far as to call for his resignation. I was in Newcastle at the time looking at one of Britain's most deprived council wards on a select committee visit. I reluctantly agreed and found a phone line to deliver the necessary call for resignation. I dreaded bumping into Keith for weeks after. Of course in the end it was fine. He'd been caught in a media storm and was understanding about what I'd said. I apologised and to this day he always gives a cheery hello and chats as we wander around work. I guess politicians can develop a thick skin, although in my case it's not thick enough. I let things get to me and worry about what I've said and what others say about me.

Another regret was a comment I made about John Prescott on the *Today* programme. It was during the summer silly season and the 'Prescott's in charge' headlines had become something of an early August tradition, right up there with the railway track melting and the first hosepipe ban. Anyway, I made some cheap jokes and remarks at Prescott's expense on the *Today* programme and joined in the general open season on the deputy PM. A few days later I was astonished to receive a private handwritten letter from Prescott. It basically told me to grow up, not to be so immature and to cut out the personal attacks. I was initially amazed that he would write a note like this, and it showed he clearly operates on a short fuse. That said, I took note and it was the last time I ever went for silly personal attacks and in a strange way I am grateful to him for the stern words.

Appearing on television programmes also involves plenty of hanging about. This takes place in the green room. Why 'green' I have no idea, as it is normally dull grey. However, the participants hang around, normally with somebody from make-up and a team of researchers and piles of newspapers. The waiting can be tedious, but on occasions it is surprising who you can meet. I think the producers must have quite a laugh to themselves to see what the oddest combination can be. I once found myself with Jeffrey Archer and Robert Kilroy Silk; it actually made even me feel quite virtuous. Most of the time you just natter and get on; there are, however, some who just won't let up and rant away. Ann Widdecombe is the worst. As the MP for Maidstone she shared the Meridian television region with me so it meant we did a number of programmes together. She would rant in the green room, rant on the set and then as I tried to escape and walk back to Westminster she would harangue me all the way. Still there was one advantage in appearing with her: I never failed to enjoy the look on the sound engineer's face when he had to try and clip the microphone somewhere onto her rather ample chest.

Screwing Up

On the whole I felt much more comfortable running round studios than sitting on the green benches. I found it intellectually easier and it raised my profile but, as I was to discover, becoming a public figure brings with it unwanted media attention that was to have disastrous consequences.

6

Hair today – gone tomorrow

As my political career progressed the press started to label me one of Westminster's young Turks but by the start of 2004 I was feeling anything but young. I think I must have hated the idea of turning forty ever since my thirtieth birthday. As the day got closer I dreamt up more imaginative ways to avoid it.

In the end I settled on a four-day trip to New York. In grumpy fashion I planned to fly back on my actual birthday so as I left JFK on the 8.00 a.m. flight there was little chance of some awful birthday surprise being sprung during the day. Family and friends had been warned to avoid the whole subject. There would be no big party and any massive banner saying 'Mark is 40' anywhere near the village would result in swift legal action.

If my birthday had been a pools or lottery ticket win the 'no publicity' box would have been firmly ticked. Why celebrate the damn thing – so that people can turn up and mock that half your life has gone? A quick look at the range of fortieth birthday cards says it all, full of pictures of fat balding men and cheap digs at getting old and losing your sex drive.

I think I started to really hate myself when I turned forty. It is a point at which you no longer feel attractive to yourself or other people. I now have more hair on my back than on my head. It's a cruel twist of nature – you spend your youth with a full head of hair then suddenly it starts to move down to your ears, nose and back. The awful moment then arrives as you have to decide what to do with all this unwanted extra hair. Belinda and her friends often threaten me with waxing. Frankly I would rather stand in Winchester High Street selling the *Socialist Worker* than have some beautician put a strip of hot wax on my back, let alone anywhere else.

If I am honest, hair loss had a big impact on me. I admitted as much in the *Sunday Times* article I wrote a few weeks after I resigned. The headlines that followed were predictable, cruel and, of course, rubbish. 'Oaten blames scandal on hair loss' was typical. It is utter rubbish to suggest that losing my hair made me go off the rails, but feeling old, of which hair loss was a very public symbol, did, in my view, play a part.

Everybody tells me that having no hair is not a problem, get over it! Well, I just find that tough. A series of photographs of me printed in the *Daily Telegraph* showed how I had gone from a full head of hair when I was elected in 1997 to a baldy by 2005.

Unfortunately on this front the camera doesn't lie and it's there for all to see, or not in my case. All this is, of course, absolutely hysterical to others and on reflection I get the funny side now. Just the word 'bald' makes people chuckle. My head has been described as a 'cricket ball' by one columnist and I will admit, before I lost my hair I would enjoy the odd slap-head joke myself.

Of course going bald is common and if your mother's father went bald the chances are that you could be heading in the same direction. My granddad had lost his hair by his mid-twenties so I guess I should be grateful I hung on to mine until I was forty. What's not that common is successful or famous baldies – Yul Brenner (dead now), Telly Savalas (dead now), William Hague and Iain Duncan Smith (both died as political leaders). Can you name me a newsreader or top politician whose head looks like a swimming cap? Exactly, there aren't any.

In fact people go to great lengths to try and hide their baldness. There is a well-known Tory politician who is rumoured to wear a wig. In the childish world of Westminster, when he stands up to speak people often shout out 'toupée'. That kind of adolescent humour abounds in Westminster and nicknames are very popular. I remember another Conservative MP who was once seen falling down drunk as he hailed a cab. He ended up with the Commons taunting of 'taxi' every time he tried to speak. John Prescott, of course, had to endure years of 'waiter' being chanted out – a reference to his time served on a cruise ship.

I have to admit that I have flirted with some of the 'natural' products that are often advertised. There is one particular one that you see on all the Underground billboards showing ex-footballer Lee Sharpe's smiling face under a mass of hair which advertises a product for hair loss. It did have me rushing to the Google search bar and trying it for a six-month period, after which I was £150 worse off without an extra hair in sight. At about the same time I was asked if I would agree to be the subject of a TV documentary to trial a new hair product but given that these things can often take months, it would hardly have been gripping TV. Then there is, of course, the Elton John approach, which if we are to believe some of the press stories involved a bit of scalpel on scalp action, but that would involve needles so is a complete no-no for me.

After a few years in office even Tony Blair started to recede, much to the fascination of the media. The lobby journalists get a great view of politicians' heads as they sit high up in the chamber of the House of Commons and look down on every Honourable Member. They alone have a unique insight into the tell-tale patch that can start monk-like at the top of your head. Worse, though, is when you're in television studios, with the harsh artificial lighting. I pray for uplighting, as it shines on your face from the ground, which means it can be quite nice and soft. Downlighting, however, is a spotlight on your baldness. Make-up artists often slap countless layers of powder on me to try and take the shine off, often having to run on stage in recording breaks and give me a top-up. One clever girl even proposed putting some eyeliner on top of my hair to try and make it look like it had thickened up!

Make-up and politicians do have a history. I remember on one occasion, when I was managing director of Westminster Public

Relations, we had secured a contract to help Mikhail Gorbachov with a book tour and speeches in the UK. After seeing him at first hand I noticed just how much make-up he had on his head in an attempt to cover his famous birth mark. It struck me as odd that the leader of the communist world wore make-up. Previous Soviet premiers wouldn't have been seen dead doing that – apart of course when lying in state.

Sadly, it was not just the loss of my crowning glory that came along when I turned forty, it was also the onset of a rather ugly belly. I used to look somewhat emaciated in holiday pictures as a teenager, now I look as if I am permanently five months pregnant! I drank and ate more then and took no exercise, but it seems to be an automatic rule that the day you turn forty, for every pint or pound you consume, it doubles and immediately ends up on your belly and chin.

All of this is highlighted when you go to buy a new suit. I hate changing rooms. They are always hot and stuffy and you have to negotiate undressing in a space that resembles the size of two tumble dryers. Then there is the three-sided mirror. Why on earth do shops do this? When you buy clothes surely the idea is to make you feel good about yourself; instead they encourage you to endure a circus-style freak show by looking at yourself from three different angles.

Of course the suit is the easiest garment to wear. For the forty-something the real problem is what you should wear to look casual, which is even worse if you are a politician. Remember William Hague and the baseball cap at the Notting Hill Carnival? During parliamentary recess the Commons is very often full of MPs dressed in casual gear. For the Conservative MPs the uniform is often a pair of brogues, chinos, a pink shirt, blue pullover and a tweed jacket.

Given half a chance I would be in jeans and a T-shirt and I would certainly be unshaven. In fact I hate having to shave and dress smartly for the television at the weekend. Before David Cameron even thought about television without ties, I was giving interviews without one, because it was more comfortable, not because I was a moderniser. A tie to me is a symbol of stuffiness. Of course around Westminster, though, not wearing a tie is unacceptable. As chair of the Liberal Democrats I would attempt to hold parliamentary party meetings without a tie. Bob Russell, the lively MP for Colchester, would often try to raise a point of order and offer to loan me his tie during the meeting.

When I ran for leadership of the party I was accused of trying to be trendy by not wearing a tie. The Ming Campbell camp was lined up with phrases about it being more important to have ideas than not to wear a tie. If truth be told they do have a point; I could certainly never have competed with the elegance of Ming Campbell. It is just beyond me how he always seems to look so polished, pressed and smart each day. My life is a constant struggle to find an ironing board and a shirt and put the two together, let alone to polish my cheap Clarks shoes. So, by default, or because I feel more at home that way, I am up for the more relaxed look.

I once did *Question Time* without having shaved for a few days. That really got the bloggers going – 'what a disgrace that he is allowed on the programme without shaving'. Why does a bit of stubble get such a lot of interest? It even made the diary pages of a couple of national newspapers – 'is the Liberal Democrat MP growing a beard?' No, I tried to protest, it is designer stubble, but then there was even a debate about when designer stubble becomes a beard. I would say about ten days in my case.

As I approached turning forty I started to find the pressure at work enormous. I was regularly feeling low about myself, my job and life in general. Self-doubt about my abilities and the ageing process, combined with a gruelling work programme, started to affect my health. I was waking up at night with chest pains and sweating, often thinking I was having a heart attack for hours on end. Although now I know they were panic attacks they felt very real and frightening at the time.

My doctor told me that the biggest underlying reason men in their thirties came to see him was ultimately stress. It was getting ridiculous in my case; I would go through a cycle of events that would nearly always lead to a medical examination to reassure myself that I was fine in the first place. In a six-year period I convinced myself that I had a brain tumour, heart problems, stomach cancer, testicular cancer, hearing loss and God knows what else. I wish I could get to read my doctor's records; they would be laughable, if rather long. Each time I would start with a slight ache and build up to more until my mind would dwell on it, initially every hour, and then I would end up thinking the worst.

I would make desperate efforts to ease my mind by having long conversations with myself: 'Come on, Mark, get a grip – pain on the right-hand side is OK, it's pain on the left-hand side you should worry about.' I would even go running for miles and push myself just to see if I would drop dead. If I didn't, I would be reassured, but that reassurance would only last for a couple of hours.

I knew I was a hypochondriac, but it made no difference because however hard I tried to rationalise things, the pain and fear felt very real. So the cycle of events went on, and I would call the doctor and make an appointment. I've been able to remember hardly any phone numbers in my life, but the one for my local surgery is embedded in my brain. I am sure the receptionist recognises my voice. Appointment secured, I would then start to build up for my meeting with the doctor and convince myself that blood would have to be taken at some point when I saw him.

My wobbly relationship with blood goes back a long way, I first remember a problem in biology lessons at secondary school with Mr Scarf, our tall, lanky, blond biology teacher. He was a kind-looking man, always wearing a long white lab coat, wandering around in between the Bunsen burners as we cut up frogs or crickets, which were kept in big jars soaked in funny-smelling fluids. I had little problem with seeing a locust torn apart and liked a good flame and test tube trick as much as the next person. It was when the focus turned to human biology that things started to go badly wrong. I am sure it would not be allowed today, but this particular morning we were issued with a small pin, a piece of glass and a microscope. It began to dawn on me that we might be examining blood through the microscope and that the blood actually I was expected to collect might actually be my own.

My school, Queens' Comprehensive, was at that time known as a 'butcher's comprehensive', code for a tough school. The rest of the class

First day at nursery school.
I am at the front, pushing what
seems to be a woolly dog.

Aged nine, with my mother.
I was mortified when she got
cancer at this time.

With Belinda, not long before we got married.

My father and stepmother with
Alice (*left*) and Milly in St Mark's
Square, Venice.

My mother-in-law is not in fact
a battleaxe; far from it.
She just doesn't like canvassers.

My mother, grandmother and uncle with Alice.

Paddy Ashdown with his very late 46th MP outside Winchester Cathedral. (*Hampshire Chronicle*)

With Charles Kennedy during the by-election campaign, freezing on a visit to a farm.

My constituents got a bit of a surprise when they saw the new dustman!

Campaigning with Don Foster and Shirley Williams – she's the most popular politician I've ever met.
(*Hampshire Chronicle*)

Roy Jenkins was one of my political heroes.
I had the privilege of meeting him on one occasion.

Ballot boxes being tampered with under my nose in Montenegro.
I was part of the Council of Europe's election monitoring team.

Visiting the European Union Force in Chad. The Polish drivers blasted us with Europop as we bounced around the desert.

You can't survive a crisis without a strong group of friends. I've known Martin (*far left*), Fizz (*centre right*) and Stuart since I was thirteen.

Another family holiday in the rain.

seemed to relish the chance to self-harm and within moments of the off Mr Scarf was overseeing a virtual bloodbath of pins stuck in fingers. It made the opening scenes of *Saving Private Ryan* seem like a Jane Austen period drama. Almost instantly I went as white as my lab coat and found myself being hauled into the corridor, missing the rest of the lesson. The postscript to the event, when my homework was returned, was Mr Scarf describing in red ink my pencilled diagram of blood cells as being 'too faint'. I always felt it would be more appropriate if he had added a K to the first word.

Throughout my schooldays I regularly had nosebleeds, which scared me and resulted in exam papers being submitted with smudged red marks followed by a trip to lie down in Matron's office – and so started the love/hate relationship with blood which has lasted to this day.

I can still remember the horror of the day that the school's BCGs took place. I think I must have been about twelve or thirteen when a decree came down from the school saying that all children should be injected with whatever it was that would stop you getting TB. We were taken form by form throughout the day to queue up in the dining room and then led down a very narrow corridor towards Matron's room, where the needles were stuck in. I can picture the queue now, like cattle being sent to slaughter, but I never made it beyond the table set aside in the dining room where the teachers ate their lunch. I remained slumped there as my classmates filed past rolling up their white shirt sleeves in eager anticipation. As a result, I have never been immunised against TB or anything else much.

That makes foreign trips a bit of a hazard: any travelling that involves the need for injections requires me to consider the merits of the visit against the list of injections involved before I even start to think about what the climate or the food may be like. On a recent appointment at St Thomas' Hospital, the nurse had to call in for extra help as I was having my arm pumped with anti-this and anti-that for a trip to Chad in central Africa.

Returning to my doctor's waiting room, it must be like every waiting room you go into. You think that you are seeing your doctor about X, but after five minutes looking at the posters warning of every single disease that has ever been written about in the *British Medical Journal* you are not quite sure whether you have got X, Y or Z, or perhaps a fatal combination of all three. By this point I am in a nervous frenzy, flicking through the magazines without registering a single word. I hate golf, but will read *Golf World*. Cars to me are either red or black, but I even find myself glancing at *Top Gear* magazine.

It's a fact of life that magazines in doctors' or dentists' waiting rooms are at least three years out of date. When the practice managers go off on their regular training courses they must be issued with Department of Health circulars that require them to create an environment which makes patients think they are three years younger than they actually are before they see anyone. And it works. In my surgery Percy Thrower is still potting out in *Gardener's World* and fox hunting is thriving in *Country Life*.

Desperate not to catch anybody's eye I continue to flick through a guide to fly fishing in the river Test, all too aware that fellow patients have begun to wonder what their MP is doing there. 'Hello, nice to see you using the NHS,' splutters one through a nasty cough. 'Not in Westminster today, then.' No, what does it bloody look like? I am sure the country won't collapse if I have one day off.

'Mark Oaten, please,' bellows Dr Stokes. Damn! My cover's been blown and every face looks up from *Horse and Hound* as I sprint out of the waiting area and make a dash for the consulting room. Dr Stokes and I go through the awkward small talk, with him asking me how things are and looking at the computer screen only to discover that I was in a couple of weeks ago.

We then discuss the latest ailment and soon I am lying down being prodded and probed, desperate for a positive sign. Then comes the inevitable blood pressure check. I hate that pumping black band round my arm. It reminds me of a holiday Belinda and I took back in the mid-1980s. We were on a Greek island and fancied doing some scuba diving. We were required to have a quick health check carried out by a rather doddery-looking Greek doctor in the depths of the boat that was going to take us offshore. When my turn came for the check-up I spent ages below deck and eventually emerged white as a sheet with the help of two of the crew, who informed Belinda that I'd passed out when my blood pressure was taken! My nuptial credentials as a wimp were firmly established from this point on.

My medical records now have a firm warning to doctors that I have a needle phobia. When blood has to be taken it's not quite a case of the doctor chasing me round the room, but more my lying flat out and demanding to talk about Watford Football Club at high speed to take my mind off things. One visit required no blood being taken, but resulted in a fair amount of head scratching amongst the GPs. I had woken up one morning to find my tongue had turned orange. Not just mild orange, but in true Liberal Democrat poster style it was DayGlo orange. It looked ridiculous. I was due to appear on *Question Time* a week later and was petrified that the camera would expose my freak tongue status. The doctors threw everything – tablets, lozenges, mouthwash – at it without success. Eventually I thought I would discuss it in confidence with one of the three Liberal Democrat MPs that were also doctors. Peter Brand, the MP for the Isle of Wight, seemed the most like a GP and, unlike Doctors Evan Harris and Jenny Tonge, still practised. Standing in the Commons car park, he took one look and said: 'Ah, the Victorians always had that, just scrape it off.' He was spot on and my tongue was quickly restored to normal.

When I finally get the all-clear my panic immediately lifts – it is just amazing. I get an adrenalin rush and feel like running out, leaving all thoughts of the surgery behind as I head towards the chemist. I make all sorts of promises to myself: OK, Mark, this is the deal, you're fine this time, take it as a warning – less drink, less work, more running and more fun. I know it's pathetic – but there you go.

Thankfully, given my fear of all things medical, I've yet to have stitches or an operation. I am clumsy, though, and regularly end up in Winchester A&E. I managed to break my collar bone when I rode an Italian ice cream seller's bike over a 10-foot ridge. As I don't normally do fun I am not sure what possessed me to jump on the damn thing but it soon became clear I had no sense of control as I hurtled head over heels, landing with the bike on top of me. Still, it gave the ambulance crew a chance to lobby me on the need for new vehicles. About six months later I managed to imbed a needle in my foot. For some reason, I trust not deliberate, Belinda had left it standing point up on the stairs. It went in one side and out the other. As I hobbled into A&E a few constituents muttered that it was good to see me using the local hospital, as if I had stuck the needle in myself to show I really do use the local services. I think I get my clumsiness from my dad. He had an unerring ability to tread in dog shit on any family trip, much to my mother's fury.

Sadly, though, there is a more serious side to my fear of doctors, one in which I am not alone. Stress-related illness is on the rise, made worse by the economic downturn and day-to-day pressures of life. Stress expresses itself via illness, but also via mental health battles. My mind never seems to rest; I seem to have a permanent running commentary taking place in my head with subtitles of my life continually moving across like the tickertape on 'Final Score'. I can't escape this dialogue with myself; it is at its most intense when I am alone and travelling, but even in company the dialogue continues, not really interrupted by conversation. Am I alone in this? Surely everybody has this sensation, but I have never heard people owning up to it, or talking about it, or describing it. At times I will dwell on it, over-analyse it and allow it to nag at me. At its most intense it is like some kind of internal Filofax, or in today's terms a BlackBerry of the brain. I want to scream out: 'Leave me alone! I just want to enjoy the moment! Stop bugging me, stop planning, and stop moving me to the next thing!' It seems to me at times I just can't enjoy the present. It's all about what's next and when I arrive at the next thing I'm immediately thinking about the thing after that.

Everybody's brain is of course ticking away. That's its job. The question is our ability to ignore its mutterings and blank them out. For me, however, I was in a job that was turning me mad. The impact that the hours were having on my health were starting to hit home and by the end of 2004 I was reaching an all-time low.

Many people working under pressure tend to think they manage well by using adrenaline as a body-made drug to keep them going. For me an early morning interview would often require a quick kick of nerves to wake me up – any speeches or events during the day would result in adrenaline to help keep the energy level up and make it look as if I were on top form.

It's common in all sorts of jobs. How often have you heard people say 'I am at my best under pressure', 'I need a rush of adrenaline' or 'I work to deadlines'? We all do it. But we are running our body in distress mode. After a few years at this pace the adrenaline actually stays with you throughout the day, not in short bursts, but constantly bubbling away. That's when the danger kicks in, that's what can lead to burn-out. The body becomes too dependent on this internal drug and it overtakes you. In medical terms the adrenal glands are not able to deal with constant stimulation and this can disrupt your immune system, leading to illness.

Adrenaline for me was a quick fix – a fire-fighting measure and a very effective way to cover up the real problems with my daily life; however, it put me on a slippery slope. In reality I was not making good decisions. There was a lack of clear thinking and it led to mistakes. I was also pushing things aside and in particular eroding relations with my family by always putting them last. It felt as if people owned me and everybody wanted to grab a bit.

Then I started to feel that my life was out of control, my career a fast-moving escalator, impossible to get off. And here is the real catch: you forget to find time for fun and relaxation, so your only form of a break or treat becomes another adrenaline rush, or risk – and that's what leads you to making crazy mistakes.

I had always come from the school of thought that said if something was wrong you just pulled yourself together. I had little time for anti-depressants or people who spent their life in therapy. How wrong I was. My frequent trips to the doctor throughout 2004 were clearly stress related and when it became clear that the solution was not medical but mental I happily agreed to seek out professional help. Since then I've seen counsellors on a regular basis and found it a great help. It's nothing like what the sitcoms portray and I've never once lain down on a couch. It's more like a focused gossip with some set rules. The sessions always last fifty minutes, you don't ask too many questions of your therapist and the whole thing is confidential. That means for one of those rare times in your life you can say what you like without fear of hearing it weeks later.

There is, however, one cliché that is true about the whole process. Before long you realise that 'Tell me about your childhood' is rather more important than you think. I'd always categorised my early years as normal and happy. Now, looking back, I have some regrets. At the time, being an only child was wonderful. I got full-on undivided attention and a first go at the bottled milk, which in those days meant the creamy gold top milk, unless the blue tits had got to it first. Now, I am not so sure about the benefits. A family of three is too small; a child needs other children to learn to play, fight and share with. Being an only child has made me shy and a loner. I find it hard to join in and need to go off and have solo time. I am sure there is loads of research on 'only child syndrome' which until recently I would have filed under B for bollocks, but the therapy has made me look at things in a different way.

Counselling became a vital part of my week until it ended in 2008. We talked about work, illness, pressure, marriage, children and *me*. I would recommend it to anybody – and particularly those heading for forty. Like it or not, this is one of those moments when you take stock. Based on the average male life expectancy, then more than half your life is gone. I defy anybody not to have at least a small wobble at this sobering prospect.

Work was not just making me ill, but was starting to take its toll on my marriage. One of the consequences of the two-vote win and then the by-election victory was that every local Liberal Democrat constituency party wanted me to speak at their annual dinner. Within weeks of my by-election victory requests were pouring in, often making very clear that they had been there to help me, and now it was time to return the favour. As a consequence 1998 proved to put enormous strain on my marriage as my weekends were taken up on the rubber chicken circuit. After the stresses of being involved in two elections in 1997 my family deserved an easier year ahead, but instead I flung myself into a gruelling schedule, criss-crossing the country on Friday and Saturday nights like a stand-up comedian, telling the story of my election to raise funds for local parties. At the same time every group and every individual wanted me in Winchester. Letters and calls would start 'It was my vote that won it, now will he come to this, speak at that, or open the other?'

The diary was a nightmare and Belinda was left wondering what I looked like. It was totally unfair. Alice was eighteen months old and I was nowhere to be seen. I would turn up at 5.00 p.m. on a Friday after surgery, dash in, run up the stairs, shower, change into my DJ and rush out, heading for some godforsaken event. By the autumn of 1998 this situation was causing serious tension in our relationship.

'I am sorry, surgery just went on and on, then the phone went and I had to sign these letters.'

'What time are you going out?'

'In twenty minutes.'

'Can't you cancel? Why do they want you? Don't they realise you have a wife and baby?'

'I can't let them down, I promised, they've sold lots of tickets.'

'You're a complete bastard, you've changed. All that counts now is this bloody job. What about me? I've been stuck here all week.'

'Look, I know, it's just bad at the moment. After next weekend it gets better, I promise.'

But it never did. The invitations kept coming in. I said no to so much and would try to remember all the things I turned down and tell Belinda so she knew, but she only saw me still disappearing, leaving her alone.

Throughout this time Belinda had a real sense of isolation and felt both rejected and deserted by me. Life was all about me and I selfishly ploughed on without showing any affection or love for her. I can see it now, but at the time your marriage can become yet another demand on your time. Everybody wants a piece of you and the mistake that I, and others, made is to allow those close to you to drop further and further down as a priority. This sounds harsh, but I felt like one of those jugglers that has to rush back and forth to keep plates from falling off a stick. My marriage was always that last plate, saved as I made it just in time to prevent it crashing down. In the end, though, it was to do just that.

7

Negotiating with Mr Blair and Mr Bean

The days and months after the terrorist attacks on London in the summer of 2005 were to place enormous demands on all of those working in and shadowing the Home Office.

On 7 July itself I woke up feeling awful – I was suffering from one of my stress-related illnesses and I'd not eaten properly in days. Moments after the bombs exploded my pager and phone went into overdrive as the awful horror of the attacks unfolded. It was clear I would need to get to Westminster urgently. With all trains cancelled I had no option but to drive in as far as I could and walk the final stretch. As I was getting close, walking along the Embankment in pouring rain, Ming Campbell covered for me in response to the urgent Commons statement from the Home Secretary, Charles Clarke.

At about five o'clock, Clarke asked if I would join him and Conservative spokesman David Davis for a meeting at the Home Office. It was to be the first of many as the three of us embarked on an attempt to keep party politics out of the fight against terrorism. Given the sensitive issues involved, we developed a strong understanding, respect and trust in the months that were to follow. The tone was set at this first meeting when we sat and watched as the horrors of the day unfolded on a large screen broadcasting into the Home Secretary's meeting room.

I was surprised at how much interest there was in watching Sky News. I'd imagined the Home Secretary would be in a situation room, surrounded by screens and with people running in and out with the latest intelligence. Instead we speculated along with everybody else and paused in our conversation to watch key developments on news channels.

Throughout my dealings with Clarke I found him warm, intelligent, on top of his brief, reasonable and understanding of my difficulties as a liberal trying to deal with some fairly draconian legislation. Davis was also straightforward in our dealings, a bit of a political bruiser who regularly joked that he would rearrange my face if I disagreed with him, but apart from that he was professional and often a more ardent defender of liberal values than I was. We all got to know each other well, often sharing a bottle of red wine as we grappled with a fast-moving set of problems that were to test us emotionally, intellectually and politically.

At times I struggled with the need to balance national security and liberal values towards civil liberties. Attending the memorial for the victims of the London attack was uncomfortable, not just because of the shared sense of emotion and loss, but because of a nagging political concern I felt. By trying to prevent new legislation on terrorism was I putting principle ahead of people's lives? This dilemma never escaped me and it was often left to lawyers in my party to remind me that our liberty was not just about protection from terrorism, but about protection of the values and principles we hold dear, which terrorists seek to undermine. Fine words, but try telling them to the relatives of somebody murdered on a London bus.

So I had some private sympathy with Clarke and Tony Blair when they announced a set of measures to tackle terrorism. In our private meetings days after the bombings took place I gave my word that I would look at any proposal with an open mind and there would be no knee-jerk opposition. The consensual approach, I said, was my preferred route. I was able to persuade Charles Kennedy that if cross-party talks took place it was absolutely vital that we joined and did not put ourselves on the sidelines objecting to measures at such an early stage. I would have resigned my position if the party had forced me to leave the talks.

The country had just faced the worst terrorist attack we'd known and I judged that despite our concerns at how Labour might respond, the public wanted to see its politicians working hard together to find solutions. Now was not the time for a political bust-up.

A week after the bombing the Home Secretary shared in confidence some of his early thoughts on what the government might do and informed me that both the Intelligence Service and the Metropolitan Police were drawing up a wishlist. Items to be considered included measures to make it an offence to prepare for a terrorist attack. In principle I was prepared to look at any of these measures and when Clarke, Davis and I held a press conference on the steps of the Home Office I made it clear that the Lib Dems would approach all discussions on the basis of finding agreement, as that was what the public would demand.

Privately, however, concerns were starting to be raised with me from Liberal Members of the House of Lords, who looked beyond the electoral consequences of our position to the legal and human rights aspects. There were many valid questions that needed asking and in our meetings I started to voice objections. But any questions were met with a sharp rebuke from Tony Blair, keen to paint Liberals as the friend of suicide bombers at the first opportunity.

Although the detail of the cross-party work was undertaken by Clarke, Davis and me, the high-profile nature of the subject meant that Blair became directly involved. Along with Charles Kennedy I met with him on two occasions at Downing Street as we were mid-way through our negotiations. Having never mixed with the Prime Minister before, I was rather surprised at the quality of small talk. Waiting around with Kennedy, Blair and Michael Howard in the backrooms of Downing Street was like being at the hairdresser's as we all discussed summer holiday plans. It was rather refreshing – normal and mundane. Meetings took place in the Prime Minister's small outer office and then on more formal occasions in the Cabinet Room. At one meeting I was astonished when Blair suddenly hit the Cabinet table and proceeded to sound off about human rights. 'It's all about other people's human rights. What about our need for people's protection?'

He looked exhausted and frustrated at the whole situation. It would be too easy to dismiss him as a man who did not care about civil liberties. To this day I am convinced that Blair genuinely felt concerned and ultimately responsible for the safety of the people he represented as Prime Minister. I am sure he feared a political backlash if a further attack took place and he'd not been seen to act tough. But what really irritated me was the suggestion that if we opposed these changes we were 'soft on terrorism'. That was simply not the case.

My argument with him was not that civil liberties should come first, but rather that the measures he was putting forward would not actually help. It seemed to me that if the Intelligence Service wanted measures in place that would make us safer then I had a duty to consider putting them ahead of civil liberty concerns, but that was not in my judgement necessary. Even when I was given intelligence briefings there was nothing I was told that convinced me.

As an example of this: at a meeting with the spooks in Charles Kennedy's office we asked them what objections they had to the use of intercept evidence to help achieve prosecutions. At the time many of us argued that we could fulfil our principles of holding trials if evidence gained from secret surveillance was allowed in court. Although not ideal it was better than holding suspects without charge for months or placing them under control orders (a way of holding individuals under a form of house arrest). The Intelligence Service response was far from convincing. They seemed to feel that it would be hard to achieve as the telecommunications giants would be reluctant to agree to data from their systems being used. It was nonsense. Of course the chairman of BT would agree if national security was involved and of course the data could be kept confidential to, say, a panel of three judges meeting in private.

I also met the head of the Metropolitan Police, Sir Ian Blair, to discuss his wishlist. Again I wasn't that convinced. I'd had a number of meetings with senior Met officers at that time, including Deputy Assistant Commissioner Brian Paddick. On one occasion Paddick asked for a private meeting and to my amazement he launched an attack on Sir Ian, and then made a series of statements about the events that followed the shooting of Jean Charles de Menezes. He seemed to imply that the Met had wanted to delay announcing that de Menezes was innocent to keep the impression that the police had indeed killed a terrorist. Paddick also went on to describe a Met Police force full of fear, bitterness and personal rivalry. I walked back from Scotland Yard appalled that our capital's police force was so clearly full of poison at the top. Paddick seemed genuinely worried by what had happened and I had no reason to doubt his word, but I felt a responsibility to pass on what I'd heard. I called a contact at the Independent Police Complaints Commission, as I knew they were investigating the de Menezes case. I passed on what I'd been told and even today I remain worried about the events surrounding that episode.

Before the summer recess the Home Secretary called one last three-way meeting to discuss the latest position on legislation. I was concerned at timings and in particular wanted to know when the government would make public its planned legislation. I had a tricky party conference speech to give in mid-September and told Charles Clarke that it was vital we knew what was planned before then. If not, Lib Dem delegates might second-guess the issues and bind me into a position with a conference vote – making the consensual approach near-impossible.

Clarke promised that nothing would be said until about a week before our conference and he certainly didn't expect any big surprises. We shared contact points and holiday plans. He was heading for America, I was off to France. Poor David Davis joked that with yet another possible Conservative leadership crisis on the way he would be spending his summer visiting constituency associations up and down the country. We left in good heart. But within days things took a turn for the worse.

I was in a restaurant looking out at the sea in St Tropez when a call came through that Home Office minister Hazel Blears needed an urgent chat with me following a call from No. 10. As I walked outside on the promenade Blears told me that Tony Blair was going to make a few pre-holiday comments on terrorism. Her words were crystal clear. 'Mark, there's nothing in there to worry you. Tony just wants to say a few things before he heads off on holiday; we just wanted to let you know.'

The next day things went berserk. My attempt to spend a day on the beach was in tatters as Blair appeared to rip apart the party consensus with a shopping list of measures that were totally unacceptable and had never formed part of the agreement between Clarke, Davis and me. As I tried to make sandcastles and put sun cream on the children with one hand whilst holding the phone in the other I became horrified at what some journalists were telling me.

Blair, at his final press conference before heading off on holiday, launched a twelve point plan on terrorism. Three controversial measures stood out. Firstly he wanted to extend the use of control orders. Secondly he planned legislation creating an offence of glorifying terrorism. Finally he was seeking to extend the period police could question individuals without charge from fourteen to ninety days. I was left with the conclusion that with Clarke away Blair and the loyal Blears had decided to give in to the Intelligence Service and put their wishes ahead of party consensus.

It was a fatal mistake and a few months later was to lead to one of the most dramatic parliamentary votes in New Labour's history. Throughout September and October opposition to the Blair proposals began to focus on the 'ninety day' measure. This became the symbol for the liberty-versus-safety debate. I guess it was one of the easier measures to understand and allowed for months of endless media discussion. Journalists speculated if I would move from fourteen days to twenty-eight, or if Clarke would shift to sixty days from ninety. It was all slightly ridiculous and quickly became a media circus. Any meeting between the three of us would result in the press pack hunting for a sign of weakness in one camp. Davis and I worked very well together, both determined not to blink first, and for my part I was acutely aware I could not be out-liberalled by him. Every choice of phrase in an interview would be analysed and if you walked out of the studio complex in Millbank you'd be surrounded by hacks trying to get the very latest.

On one occasion in mid-October, I sensed that Davis was wobbling on ninety days and said so live on BBC News. He was in a studio on the floor above, probably doing Sky News, but heard what I said. As I left he confronted me: 'If you say that again I'll smash your nose in.' I think he was cross! But it demonstrated how difficult it was to carry out negotiations in private rooms and TV studios at the same time. As if that was not colourful enough, the drama had another player. Liberty, the then little-known human rights group, had a chief executive called Shami Chakrabarti. Within a year this small, intelligent, determined fighter was to become a household name. Throughout the summer recess she had been putting enormous pressure on David Davis and me to hold our nerve on ninety days. Her tactics were a combination of intelligent briefing and brute force. On one occasion she called me from the Central Lobby demanding a meeting, saying she would refuse to leave until I saw her to explain my position on something.

Debate moved from TV studios and Home Office briefing rooms to the seaside for the party conference season. Amidst the charged atmosphere of the party faithful our messages ended up less consensual and there was a fair amount of political knockabout. In my keynote speech I said that Clarke's heart was not really in ninety days. 'Underneath there is a liberal fighting to get out; after all, he has a beard.' Funny stuff but when Parliament returned to debate the issue weeks later nobody was laughing. It was clear that the ninety-day plan was close to being defeated in a Commons vote. Last-minute deals were discussed in endless phone calls but as we worked late into the night it became clear that if the Conservatives and Lib Dems held firm we could win the vote, especially if we had the help of a considerable number of Labour rebels – many of whom had been on the receiving end of a 'Shami lecture'. By the week of the vote I was shattered and fell ill again. I could hardly hold down any food and felt unable to get out of bed. It was a disastrous time to get struck down and added to speculation that my heart was not really in opposing ninety days. Charles Clarke called me and asked if it was a diplomatic sickness. By the day of the debate and vote I felt so bad I asked Belinda to call the whips and say I could not make it. Thankfully the Kennedy office stepped in. They knew this would be disastrous for me and they sent Kennedy's advisor Olly Kendall and my researcher Owen Braben to literally haul me out of bed and drive me into Westminster. Thank God they did. In a dramatic debate and vote the government lost by just one vote; I'd had a close shave and although I was congratulated for my handling of the terrorism issue, deep down I knew it had raised both intellectual and mental health doubts, which I needed to tackle.

Screwing Up

The home affairs portfolio was demanding and in particular the 2005 election campaign was frantic. Home affairs issues were top of the agenda and I was being pushed from one election special to the other. I'd agreed to take part in a BBC programme where you were grilled by members of the public for forty minutes then given your score at the end. This particular form of political combat was due to take place in Newcastle. I was running extremely late for my flight leaving Southampton. As I attempted to rush through customs and security there was the usual banter about the election from the security officers. I explained I was in a rush to catch a plane to do a programme on crime and terrorism. 'Ah yes, terrorism – can we just look into your case?' 'Nothing to worry you in there,' I responded. In fact a couple of things had shown up on the scanner and to my utter horror a penknife and strange silver object were removed and plonked in front of me. My explanation just made things worse. The penknife was a gift from the hotel I had stayed in for Charles Kennedy's stag night and I must have put it into my briefcase months before. 'Ah, Kennedy's stag night, I see,' said the man in the yellow security jacket. 'Now – what is this silver thing?' By now they were issuing last calls for my flight and I honestly had no idea what this silver thing was until, with embarrassment, I recognised it as an electric nasal hair clipper Belinda had given me ages ago. So in hushed tones I confessed: 'It's a nasal hair thingy.' 'A what?' 'Yes, I'm sorry – look, keep it all, I've got to rush.' So much for a shadow Home Secretary's sense of airport security!

For most of the campaign I found myself on the back foot, under attack for Liberal policies from the Conservatives. In particular, my plans to allow some prisoners the right to vote provoked an outcry. They produced large billboards with my photo claiming 'This man wants to give Ian Huntley the vote'. (Huntley had killed two children a few years earlier in a horrendous attack.) It was never my intention that those serving life should vote, but for those that were soon due back into society I felt it was part of their civil duty to be encouraged to vote, just one aspect of rehabilitation.

The state of our prison system became an issue I cared a great deal about. I quickly met with the various prison reform groups and then visited some penal establishments. What I saw and some of the figures alarmed me: high levels of suicides, self-harming and mental health problems; the disgrace of a reoffending rate of over 60 per cent and the failure of a system to match punishment with any effective education or training. But reforming the system was hardly a vote winner as most polls indicated the electorate was of the 'lock 'em up and throw away the key' school of thought.

I set about developing some new policy ideas and went to Holland to look at their prison system. At one prison my researcher Olly and I were shown around by the governor. After about forty minutes I whispered to Olly that it was odd we had not seen a single prisoner. Eventually I challenged the governor about the missing inmates. 'Oh, that's normal. They all get picked up at 9 a.m., go to work and will be dropped back at 5 p.m.' A fascinating approach which was also matched with a strong education and training programme. The results were impressive: a reoffending rate well below the UK level. As the governor explained, 'If you do something meaningful with them, you will get a meaningful response.'

I became convinced that my party should set out a radical change for prisons. I called for a nine-to-five working day, getting prisoners out of their cells and into the classroom. Because I wanted this to be hard edged, I was determined that we should link any early release dates with participation in education programmes. For too long this kind of 'liberal' approach had been portrayed as 'soft on crime'. In fact, I argued, it was soft to just let a prisoner lie in a cell reading the *Daily Mirror* all day long – when the real tough option was to get them to learn to read and write (the average prisoner has a reading age of eleven).

For much of my time as home affairs spokesman the issue of ID cards was the hot topic of debate. It was a tricky one for me in the early stages. I had totally forgotten that back in 1998 I'd actually voted for an ID card scheme when the issue came to a division under what's called a ten-minute rule bill (basically a small bill which has no chance of becoming law). Anyway, the government research department didn't have to dig that far to drag it up, which the then Home Secretary, David Blunkett, was quick to point out when we had our first exchange over the issue on the floor of the House. It was embarrassing but I was able to point out that Tony Blair had voted against it in the past – so we'd both changed our minds, the difference being that I'd changed mine in the right direction. My second problem was trying to persuade the Lib Dems on the best way to campaign against the ID cards. By nature the party wanted to focus on the civil liberties implications. I was less keen on this approach. It seemed to me that we needed to appeal beyond the 'Liberty' voters and try to persuade the 80 per cent who were in favour of ID cards that they were wrong. You could never win this group over by claiming human rights – after all, they would claim their right to safety and immediately retort that if you've got nothing to hide, what's the problem?

My judgement was that the government's case was weak on a number of other strands and we should explore these. In the end we were able to create a powerful argument against. By careful use of parliamentary questions we discovered that the cost of implementation would run into millions and the actual fee for an average family would be about £100. The database would be unlikely to work or be safe and the biometrics had failed in the trials: if you were a farmer, for example, fingerprints were hard to trace. At every level the case was not made and I am glad that during the years I was in the job I played my part in shifting public opinion so that the majority of voters ended up doubtful that ID cards would work or keep them safer.

The issues surrounding ID cards were fairly simple to grasp but, to be brutally honest, some of the other bits of legislation did my head in. I had an incredibly able advisor in Tim Colbourne and he would often have to explain things for hours but they were still beyond me. I am not sure if I just panicked when I saw complex human rights legislation or if I was just too lazy or knackered to actively grasp it. In reality I would often wander into meetings, ask Tim to give me just two things to remember and then bluff my way through. The problem was that the people I was meeting could smell my lack of depth a mile off. I would be bounced from Shami Chakrabarti on the phone, to the Home Secretary, a leading lawyer, Sir Ian Blair and David Davis – it was hard to keep up and know who to believe at times. Without the intellectual confidence to argue back in debates I often attempted to take on the man-in-the-street role. So I often asked a dumb question and boiled complex issues down to a language I could grasp.

I soon realised that the lawyers and human rights groups talked in riddles, unable to deliver a sentence without reference to an act of Parliament or case law. In fact, things were not as complicated as they made out but I just lacked the confidence to take them on. For my researchers it must have been a nightmare as they attempted to brief me on control orders, incitement to religious hatred and acts purporting to terrorism.

Strangely one of the best briefings I had was from Mr Bean. Rowan Atkinson was concerned that legislation on religious hatred might impact on comedians' ability to laugh at religion. Jokes about vicars and rabbis were commonplace and western culture is used to mocking itself – but the ability to laugh at imams and Muslims was untested. If Atkinson and others wanted to make fun of this and other religions, would they be inciting hatred? We met to discuss the issues and he made powerful and indestructible arguments about freedom of speech and expression. When I told my children I'd met Mr Bean they were furious I hadn't got his autograph and very surprised he could actually talk!

I blame my failure to understand clever lawyers on my time at Nascot Wood Junior School. Situated in Watford, in the heart of the middle-class commuter belt, my classmates, all starting out in 1970, were a friendly and well-brought-up lot. Apart from a slight run-in with the school bully, I can't remember a single bad experience. The head teacher had a rather worrying habit of sitting me on his knee in his office but the school was a happy start to my education. I can remember long, hot days doing very little as we spent our afternoons cleaning out the rabbit hutch rather than reciting our five times table. The trendy laid-back 'let them express themselves' style of education may have resulted in a more articulate and vocal generation but it did nothing for my ability to learn or retain knowledge.

I may have managed to tie a pair of pyjamas in the water to create a lifejacket but if you had asked me to solve some basic mathematical equations I would have been lost. In fairness I've not needed either skill in my life. A calculator has taken care of the algebra stuff and I have not been thrown into the sea wearing just a pair of pyjamas – not yet anyway.

I deeply regretted my lack of education and in particular some knowledge of Latin, which would have helped with the lawyers, but at Queens' Comprehensive, my secondary school, there was little demand for or interest in it. However, my hatred of jargon and legal one-upmanship did, I hope, allow me to go on the *Today* programme and news channels to explain things in a simple way and at least I felt I was performing this part of my job well. In the chamber itself, my deputy, David Heath, always did a splendid job. A great Commons performer, he knew everything in great detail and we worked best when I could sit in a TV studio and he sat on the green benches.

The home affairs job gave plenty of opportunities to jump in and out of studios commenting on the latest immigration, drug or crime figures. There were also a number of incidents which flared up; I'm thinking in particular of the time when protestors threw flour at Tony Blair during Prime Minister's Questions. The flour episode was one of a number of embarrassing breaches of security at the House of Commons.

Hunting protestors managed to enter the Chamber and the pressure group Fathers4Justice climbed Big Ben and broke into Buckingham Palace. The leader of F4J, Matthew O'Connor, turned out to be one of my constituents. I didn't know this at the time and rather naively agreed to meet him in Portcullis House, the modern shopping mall-style building next door to the House of Commons. As we discussed access to children over a cuppa, I gradually became aware of a few odd stares in my direction. As I concluded the meeting and O'Connor left I was immediately approached by the head of security.

'Mr Oaten, do you know who that was?'

'Um, yes, a constituent,' I explained.

'No, that was the leader of Fathers4Justice. We've had several undercover police positioned around the building – please don't ask him again.'

Thankfully he didn't handcuff himself to me or turn into Spiderman but it was all slightly embarrassing.

Part of the home affairs job involved going out to visit police forces, prisons and crime hot spots. I did my fair share of visits all around the UK, but going to see how they did things abroad was fascinating. I went to Madrid to witness for myself how the city had put itself back together after the bombing. On that occasion it was a scorching day, with temperatures hitting 36 degrees when I arrived at the memorial in the main station. Visiting diplomats were asked to sign a book of condolence, but to my horror I realised that on this occasion you had to type your message direct into a computer, which was then displayed above on an enormous screen for all to see as you wrote. When writing, I can often disguise my dyslexia by scrawling, but this time there was no escape as I desperately struggled to figure out how to spell 'condolence' as my fingers sweated away on the keys. I was moved at the way the city of Madrid had bounced back from the terrorist attacks.

In 2004 I fixed up to see what Mayor Rudy Giuliani had achieved with his zero tolerance policy in New York. As a liberal I was always keen that we should learn of effective measures even if they looked a bit tough or right wing from the outside. For this trip I took my researcher Owen Braben. A Southport lad, he was to become a wonderful researcher and I now count him as a close mate. He hates party politics but loves the political world and I am delighted that his career has taken him from an intern in my office to working for ITN. I am convinced he will go far. However, his eyesight is not that great. On Second Avenue we were trying to catch a taxi when he managed to flag down a police car instead!

We managed to link up officially with the NYPD and spent a day with a team of tough cops, which made me keep wanting to hum the *Hill Street Blues* music – 'Let's be careful out there,' I told Owen. Their work was tough with homicides, drugs and violent crime part of the daily beat in Manhattan. But we also saw a different side to zero tolerance: on the one hand the mayor was very tough on minor crime and had cleared up Times Square, but on the other he was also keen to invest in education and training projects for those that could end up in a life of crime. We went to an education academy that was targeted at kids from poor backgrounds. Watching them struggle through the gym routine in their floppy tracksuits was amusing but the massive reduction in crime was impressive. It made me think that tough measures can have a liberal slant and I started to develop some new thinking.

It was not just on prisons and ID cards that the Liberals had allowed themselves to be portrayed as weak. In fact, the very word 'liberal' had become a synonym for weakness, soft wishy-washy ideas from people that don't live in the real world. It was from these thoughts that I came up with the idea of 'Tough Liberalism'. I argued that the Liberal approach was in fact not a soft option but in many cases harder to achieve and with a better long-term outcome. I illustrated by pointing out that offering a prisoner lessons in reading and writing was a liberal thing to do – but forcing him to do the lessons and linking a release date to his willingness to learn was tough and more effective than other measures. That was Tough Liberalism – and it worked in a range of policy areas.

The press loved it, but the party hated it and it was to be a growing sore in my relations with party activists. They wished to portray me as some right-winger and never felt at ease with what I was trying to achieve. It was just another episode in mistrust that had started not long after I was elected. The activists had been wonderful in supporting me in the by-election, but things went downhill when the small band of idiots that run the *Liberator* magazine decided to write nasty pieces about me. Their main focus of hate was a group I'd helped establish called Liberal Future. Along with a number of colleagues I was becoming frustrated at the 'nanny state' approach the party was taking. It was not very liberal on a number of issues from the ridiculous idea of wanting to ban goldfish as prizes at fairs to a very anti-private sector stance on public services. The debate within the party, in particular at party conferences, was often one-way traffic. So working with a dozen or so bright party members, many of whom worked in public relations, we established Liberal Future to try and argue for more traditional and genuine liberal policy, in some ways looking back to the Jo Grimond era.

At the same time I'd also been asked by Charles Kennedy to set up a group aimed at supporting former Conservatives that were joining the party. The Peel Group, named after the nineteenth-century Tory-turned-

Liberal Robert Peel, met occasionally and was designed to provide some back-up for the former Tory MEPs and councillors who were in need of some help to integrate into the party. We also used it to share intelligence about others that might be on the verge of joining. Hugh Dykes, the former Tory MP, and John Stevens, a somewhat maverick ex-Tory MEP, were the most active and I helped drive it forward. It had absolutely nothing to do with policy, nor was it a secret body with a right-wing plot, but again the activists were not happy. I spent years dealing with insulting emails and remarks on the party's internal chat site called CIX. Rumours even flew around that my mother was a Tory councillor when, in fact, she was a Lib Dem. They had me pigeonholed as some rich public school PR guy from a Hampshire farming family who'd just entered politics in 1997. The boy from a Watford comp elected as a councillor at twenty-two was lost on them and, to this day, I feel sad at the small group of activists that made things so rough for me with the party.

As the Lib Dem home affairs spokesman I was expected to dash around the country trying to support local Lib Dem parliamentary candidates with a visit and a press event. This normally involved a long drive, and then a mad dash to find the meeting point based on some flimsy directions from the local chairman. I'd eventually arrive bursting for a pee to be welcomed by a dozen or so local councillors, a trainee journalist from the local paper and a sulky photographer. The visit would often centre on a meeting with the local police to discuss crime and a tour of troublesome areas or some new hi-tech crime-catching gadget.

I would spend about two hours there before heading off to the next constituency. The aim was to try and fit as many winnable seats in on one regional tour. I hardly ever took along a researcher as the London crowd hated going out and about. Owen in particular refused to meet party activists unless absolutely necessary although that was no great loss – he was bloody useless at directions. On one occasion we had left Westminster to do an annual dinner somewhere east of Cambridge. Running late we raced from the underground car park below the Houses of Parliament and hit the road heading roughly in the direction of north London. By about Harlow I thought it was time to work out where we were heading only to discover Owen had put the file with directions, venue and contact names on the top of the car when he'd got in, and they were no doubt scattered over North London now. We made it to the village hall about an hour late and I ended up being given a rubber chicken and a grilling on why I had not voted on this and that.

I still don't know why I never got a satnav for my car rather than spending hours driving around the country. There was never enough time to get from A to B and in October 2004 I managed to pick up two speeding fines on the same day as I was running late to meet police in Cornwall and Devon. In fact, my licence was very nearly taken away from me due to the amount of points from speed cameras. When I reached twelve points I was offered the choice of going to court or attending a one-day course on driving skills. I was furious – every single one of my fines was for speeding below 40mph. I imagined the day would be full of boy racers all caught doing over the ton. In fact, it was nothing of the sort; all ten on the course had been caught at just under the 40mph mark and it was a well-run event that made you think again. We all trundled off on the A303 after our day's training and you've never seen a convoy of cars driven so carefully – it was about twenty minutes before anybody had the nerve to go over 30!

I am not the only Oaten to have speeding issues. Back in the summer of 2004 I was involved in the launch of the Hampshire Safety Camera Partnership and to publicise this I spent a morning in the back of a detector van pointing the camera at cars heading towards me. The local TV station came along to film it all and that night Hampshire residents must have been reassured that their MP was on the case with speeding top of his agenda. Meanwhile on the same day Belinda had other ideas. About two in the afternoon she phoned me in tears having been arrested by the police for driving at over 103mph. Bloody hell! How could her car even do that? I calmed her down and thankfully the press never made the connection between these two events. Neither of us is proud of speeding and we actually try to drive very carefully. In this job I have seen the impact of death on the road and it's not a laughing matter. Our various run-ins with the police have, I hope, acted as a good warning to us both.

8

Ego

Running alongside the political pressures of the London bombings and terrorism legislation was the start of a changing political landscape. Michael Howard had successfully stopped the rot in Tory Party fortunes, but made way for a new generation of leader shortly after the 2005 election. The arrival of David Cameron onto the political stage was to have a dramatic impact on the Conservatives' fortunes and it raised several questions over the ability of the Liberal Democrats to make progress in Tory-held seats. It had long been the case that Conservative leaders, William Hague, Iain Duncan Smith and to some extent Michael Howard, would come and go without shifting Tory support from the low 30s. The 'nasty' party looked doomed to a period of opposition, allowing Kennedy and his anti-Iraq War party to make gains from both Labour and Conservatives. Cameron, despite his traditional Conservative roots, was in my judgement a different animal. He looked and sounded more normal and with his tie-off, cycle-riding, non-stuffy approach he was a clear threat. His early policy announcements showed a willingness to take on the Tory old guard. A more relaxed approach on same-sex adoption, promoting female candidates and talking about the environment were not what you expected from a Tory.

His new leadership came at a time when I felt deeply fed up with my own political position. The Kennedy situation was going from bad to worse and his lack of activity was creating a vacuum in policy development. I felt stuck in my home affairs portfolio, clear in my mind that we should be presenting what I had described as a Tough Liberal approach. But the party at large was never really up for this and mistrusted, or in some cases deliberately misinterpreted, what I was saying.

I felt frustrated at Charles's leadership and out of kilter with a party that just never warmed to me. The party conference of 2005 brought things to a head. Despite getting great press reviews for my keynote speech and giving over twenty fringe talks I just felt that party delegates were out to get me and dismiss whatever I said, as if I was some sort of right-wing maniac.

I began to give thought to what it would be like to join the Conservatives. I would become a hate figure in my party, but I felt that many of my constituents were natural Conservatives at heart and might understand. I was close to picking up the phone to Cameron's office on a number of occasions. At times when things were really bad in the party I even discussed the pros and cons with a couple of friends. They argued against and said that trying to fight for my views in the party should be the priority. They felt I should focus on either sorting out the Kennedy problem or bringing things to a head.

One friend not involved in politics summed it up in a different way: 'Look, Mark, you've supported Watford all your life and in every division. Could you imagine supporting another team?' Strangely, amidst all the political doubts, this comparison with football tugged at my emotional connection with being a Liberal. I had joined the SDP at eighteen and I've been part of the Lib Dems in one form or another for all of my adult life. I don't think I could be anything other than Liberal and despite my frustrations with the party, so many of its members have been loyal to me and its heart is definitely in the right place. At the end of the day the Conservatives will always be just that – conservative. There can only be one radical liberal party and deep down I knew that was where I belonged. The temptation of crossing the floor disappeared and I settled on a course of action that would end in running to try and lead the Liberal Party in a post-Kennedy era. I had no desire to trigger any leadership election despite my frustration with Charles – I wouldn't wish him any harm or plot against him – and in any case I needed years more experience if I was to stand for leadership. I had assumed that Charles would go on to fight another election, giving me plenty of time to decide if I really wanted a shot at becoming leader. In the event things ran out of control and came to a head within months.

The period leading up to the Kennedy resignation was uncomfortable for all concerned. I can honestly say that the parliamentary party were on the whole a close bunch and there were never very serious issues between us. However, towards the end of 2005 there was upset and tension for many of us, with divided loyalties for those close to Charles as we saw that events were tumbling out of control. For the most part this all went on behind the scenes with meetings in corridors or a Tea Room chat rather than any formal showdown. However, eventually things came into the open. At one regular shadow Cabinet meeting Charles made a 'put up or shut up' speech and bit by bit members of the shadow Cabinet decided not to shut up. It was the Romsey MP, Sandra Gidley, who spoke first and gave the others courage to voice concerns. I've no idea if this was orchestrated, I suspect not, but it was clear that Charles was in deep trouble. Both Lembit Öpik and I spoke up for Charles, offering unconditional support – we were noticeably the only members of the shadow Cabinet to do so. The discussion concluded with a suggestion that colleagues with concerns should go and see either Charles or the chief whip, Andrew Stunell, within the next twenty-four hours. The men in grey suits had been given the opportunity to sit on the green sofas in the leader's office and face the boss. What followed was a muddle of meetings with ultimatums, and promises of action on drinking, but it did little more than buy time for Charles. It was the beginning of the final phase of his leadership.

The end came over the Christmas of 2005. I was in Austria skiing with my family when Daisy Sampson, ITV's political reporter, called to ask me about his drinking. I denied absolutely everything and she repeated my comments without giving me a tough time. It was a bizarre conversation as we both went through the motions of knowing that I was lying and knowing that she knew almost everything herself, for Daisy had worked as Charles's press advisor. I think it's to her great credit that she kept this in confidence for so long until other sources confirmed details. Others are less charitable about Daisy but from my viewpoint she's not a nasty person and was very fond of Charles.

As we spoke it was minus 8 degrees and I was wandering about outside a restaurant with snow falling all around. My teeth were chattering due to a combination of freezing weather and fear that if the Kennedy story broke, my political future would be up for grabs. That New Year in Austria was one of the worst ever. We had decided to have a family break and I ruined it by spending every hour on my mobile phone; even in the ski bubble I was on the phone trying to work out how to keep Kennedy alive for a bit longer. It was an all-time low in my treatment of Belinda and the girls. Simple pleasures like making a snowman and sledging were interrupted by my ego obsession with political developments in London and the constant calls from journalists. How on earth I ever put politics ahead of rolling around in the snow with Milly and Alice I just don't know, but I did. I would make a snowman with one hand and talk to journalists with the other. My obsession was to charge up my phone and not keep up with my family. I'd give anything now to go back to that mountain and just have fun with the kids, but at the time I was so wrapped up in events I totally lost touch with reality. I deeply regret my actions at that last family break, but at the time the whole Kennedy world was collapsing and I was not aware that my own world was about to change forever. Little did I know what a disaster that change would bring!

The Saturday Charles resigned was a day full of tears amongst those close to him. It felt unreal and was a moment we could all see coming but never felt would arrive. I'd flown back early, leaving the family to continue their holiday, and travelled to Westminster at Charles's office's request. I went to party HQ to be on the doorstep when he arrived. As he started his resignation speech I caught his press chief, Jackie Rowley, crying and that triggered me off as I gave her a hug. Some MPs were desperate to get in camera shot as Charles left. I hate all that pushing yourself in and hung back with the Kennedy team before doing a round of television interviews on the street outside. It was hard to focus. I muttered about his leadership and the need to let him have some space to sort himself out but in the cruel world that is politics no sooner had his car left the tarmac outside Cowley Street than the question turned to who would replace him. I was asked if I was going to stand and did my best to dodge the question. I'd actually got no idea or plan in place. The day before I'd been skiing and this had all come to a head way before I was ready.

I was asked to go back to Charles's house in Kennington where a small group had gathered for what felt like a wake. Charles and his wife Sarah did their best to keep spirits up but everyone around knew it was the end of an era and of our working relationships together. Charles urged me to stand for the leadership, as did many of the Kennedy team, and by now the various TV pundits had me firmly on a list which included Ming Campbell and Simon Hughes. In these moments you tend to look at what the political commentators say as an indication of your own chances and by Saturday night the press seemed favourable enough. The Sunday papers continued to speculate about my prospects and a steady stream of emails and phone calls made me realise this was a serious prospect.

Ming Campbell was quick to declare his position and by Monday the story had moved towards speculation of a coronation, which would allow him as deputy leader to take over unchallenged. I was uncomfortable with this, in part because I felt the party members should decide via an election, and also as I was not convinced that Ming would ever escape the 'caretaker' label. I felt after years of Kennedy in action on so many fronts we needed a new agenda. My ego was also getting to me. It was flattering to have speculation about my position and some bookmakers were even suggesting I could be the favourite if I ran. In the back of my mind I felt that if I didn't run now my time might never come. It's almost like an out-of-body experience. You suddenly see countless pictures in papers and articles saying you could be leader of a political party. Your friends text, family call and cab drivers have a view but at heart you're still plain old you – a boy from Watford out of his depth.

Throughout the Monday the number of emails coming to my office grew as activists urged me to stand and create an election. The Kennedy team was horrified at the prospect of a coronation, believing it would simply reward those who had plotted against Charles. Pushed on by the activists, the media and the Kennedy office, I found myself getting drawn into the idea of running – but there was one major obstacle. To run you needed support from MPs – seven to be precise. Amidst all the calls there was not a single offer of support from my parliamentary colleagues other than Charles, who could not go public, and good old Lembit.

I quickly drew on my old colleagues in Liberal Future and sought out views from this team. We met in my Westminster office on Monday and Tuesday to look at the options. I had some of the best corporate strategists and communications advisors you could hope for, many working on high street brands and used to taking tough decisions, but it was clear this was not a straightforward prospect. None of us could see an easy path to winning but felt that we could give Ming a good run for his money – and who knew what could happen if we gained support? The other, more cautious, option was to agree to back Ming and hand him the coronation as we were convinced that Simon Hughes would only stand if I triggered the contest.

It was a reminder that politics is like no other business. In corporate communications you can advise chief executives and make a fortune but nothing can prepare you for the peculiarity of a leadership election.

I hate dithering and was aware that the longer I waited the more it looked like a sign of weakness. I went over and over everything in my mind, alone and then with Owen, my researcher. At one point I said to Owen: 'Right, this is it. We're going to walk round the block and decide this once and for all.' As we were half-way round the gardens near Embankment Station this middle-aged guy came running up. 'Hi Mark, I think you're great, you've got to stand. I used to be in—' and then he named one of the biggest bands of the 1980s. I could hardly believe it. This musical icon knew me. Was this a message – so was the 80s pop singer (whose identity I've hidden) the bizarre final element that pushed me to stand?

Looking back at these forty-eight hours of indecision, I find it remarkable that I never thought if I actually wanted to do the job – if I had the answer would have been no. I had never thought about the skeletons in the cupboard or that running would suddenly trigger a news editor on a national newspaper to check out that old file marked 'Oaten' and 'affairs'.

Belinda had been fully behind whatever decision I came to – she hated the job and the hours but was also aware this was in my system and she was not going to hold me back. She was also cross at the amount of time I'd spent supporting Charles so in part felt that if I was going to kill myself it might as well be for my own leadership and not somebody else's.

We hardly had time to discuss events as things moved so fast, but once I'd made my mind up I called her and asked if she could make it to London. I then told the team and we immediately sprang into action. I'd also decided out of courtesy to go and tell Ming before it became public. I went to his Portcullis House office and explained I would announce the next day that I was running against him. True to form he was a total gentleman. I am full of admiration for the man. He is decent, intelligent and wise and despite the rumours about his attacks on Charles, he was loyal for years until I think he felt he had a duty to the party, himself and indeed Charles to voice concerns. I know from our private conversations during the Kennedy years just how torn he was. We all struggled to do the right thing and it stretched our principles to the edge of what was reasonable. Ming has always been supportive towards me and I deeply regret that when I was in his office that afternoon it was not to offer him my full support as leader.

We decided to tip off the nationals that night, saying that Oaten was due to make an announcement the next day. This had the desired effect of catching the ten o'clock news bulletins and set us up for the next day.

I was exhausted and petrified. There was no going back. The next morning Belinda opened the Velux window in the bathroom at the top of our flat in Vauxhall and slammed it shut pretty fast when she saw a camera crew outside. The leadership campaign had already started even before any official announcement. The actual announcement was a bit of a media scram. We'd chosen the entrance of a new hotel about a mile from Westminster and Belinda and I walked with supporters to meet the press. Right from the off things went wrong. The media complained they had been stuck in a wind tunnel and although my words came out well enough it was a mistake not to take questions. I was then rushed away to do a few lines from Millbank, the Westminster base for all the news channels. It felt OK at the time but the write-ups the next day were awful. One of our MPs, Phil Willis, a blunt-speaking guy from Harrogate, phoned to tell me that the launch was a disaster and he could never back me. Despite that things were so bad I still had him down as a probable!

My platform was built around the concept of a 21st-century Liberal. I argued that our party had been out of power for a century and it was time to end that with a more aggressive and robust relaunch of Liberal values. We needed to do what old Labour had done. I wanted to rebrand the word 'Liberal' so it stood for strong values – not weak wishy-washy sandal-wearing irrelevance. I argued that most people in their day-to-day lives were liberal and it was time they voted Liberal with a capital L.

Money, or lack of it, quickly became a problem. I was running around too much to understand what was going on but as we moved toward daily meetings I soon realised that our lack of a donor was a major hurdle. Leaflets, staffing, office, phones, websites all had to be set up and whilst we would all chip in I needed £20,000 fast. I now understand how the candidates running to be Labour deputy leader got into such difficulty not declaring donors. I don't think their mistakes were deliberate – it's just that the pace that things move at means it is impossible to know everything that is going on.

Day by day I did the media interviews, we built up a campaign team and a network of party supporters, we spoke to fund raisers and I did my best to keep on top of the home affairs work. But the area we could not budge was the lack of MPs. You would fix to talk to a colleague and they would cancel or not turn up. By now Simon Hughes had entered the race and was also struggling to get support – but the real surprise and killer blow was when the Eastleigh MP Chris Huhne announced he was running. As he was a newly elected MP it was a surprise and it soon became clear why I'd not firmed up on some possible supporters when they all appeared at the Huhne campaign launch!

Things were desperate by now. With the deadline approaching to get the nominations in our whole campaign focused on trying to get MPs on board. Lembit was brilliant. He kept on and on at colleagues and eventually got the seven names but only by persuading them they could still nominate me even though they would publicly declare for another candidate. Hardly a great endorsement.

By the weekend I was starting to go off the whole damn thing. I'd spent Friday night with Owen writing a speech for the first hustings and as we drove to London early on Saturday morning I was dreading facing party members at the London School of Economics. I wanted to do my speech without notes, walking around the stage – in the end I had to settle for a bit of walking then returning to the lectern. I could not shine but held my own. In the first TV debate I felt much more comfortable and wished the whole thing could be settled with a four-way debate. Instead the party set in place an eight-week marathon which involved candidates having to go all over the country. It sounded like a long-drawn-out combination of an annual dinner, party conference and the rubber chicken circuit – my idea of hell.

By week two I was seriously in trouble and spent most of Monday and Tuesday contemplating how to withdraw. Events seemed to change from hour to hour. I ended up worrying about winning and losing issues in the next five minutes rather than seeing a larger picture. Stuck in this cycle of ever-changing circumstances it became impossible to take rational decisions. Some of the bookies still had me as favourite but the word was speeding around Westminster that I could not get the nominations. Then things all went badly wrong.

Thursday morning was awful. We woke to a story in the *Independent* that had details of private emails between me and the Kennedy office. The leaked documents showed that I was short of the seven names needed to run for leader and we were asking Charles to add his name in private. These leaks were disastrous and showed just how fragile my campaign was. Charles had been very supportive of my decision to run and wanted me to run but as the outgoing leader he would not make this public. The leaks showed how messy this whole situation was and I knew it was the beginning of the end. I had no idea how the emails had been obtained but the day before my wallet had also been stolen from my desk. It was very strange and to this day I am not sure if the tabloids were fishing around or if there was some political insider creating a problem. All I do know is my wallet ended up being sent to me a week later in a brown envelope and the leaked emails were the final nail in the coffin of my leadership bid.

I had to make a decision on what to do after this damaging leak. Although I could just about muster the seven names needed to be nominated I could see little prospect of winning or having a good leadership campaign if I was constantly being asked why hardly any MPs were supporting me. To be a leader you need to have the support of at least half your colleagues and I fell way short of that. The leaks in the *Independent* exposed just how weak my level of support was. My campaign team were split on what to do. Some felt this was just a bad day and once I got to the hustings we could gain some momentum. But there had been too many bad days since I declared. My heart had not been in this from the start and now my head could catch up! I made a final decision to give up and agreed to issue a short statement late on Thursday afternoon that I was withdrawing from the contest due to lack of support. This was the only reason. I had absolutely no idea that a national newspaper was about to expose me. There had been no warning, no deal that I would step down or any last-moment attempt on my part to kill the story. I simply had no chance of winning and not enough support. So as I headed home for Winchester that Thursday night it was with a great sense of relief. The burden of ambition over. The start of a more relaxed life ahead. How wrong I was.

9

Prozac and paparazzi

Having withdrawn from the leadership contest on Thursday evening I felt wonderfully free during Friday and met with some close friends in the early evening to make plans for holidays and the future. Later on I gave a reflective after-dinner talk to the local golf club in Alresford and came home optimistic about a future away from the greasy pole of politics.

The events of Saturday morning, from the moment I opened the curtains to see the journalists to my scrambling over my back garden fence, were awful, but in a strange way they all happened so fast there was little time to think. It would be the days, months and even years ahead that would be tougher to come to terms with.

As the car sped me to the relative safety of remote Padstow I realised I had about six hours before this story would become public. I decided to call a few close friends to warn them what was coming. They were all amazed and had no idea I would ever have done anything like this. I apologised and thankfully all of them said it would not affect our friendship and offered help and support. It was a relief to know that I would still have friends to turn to. I don't find making close friends easy but I have kept in contact with a small group of friends from school and they mean a great deal to me.

Screwing Up

Martin was my best man, and although we have less in common these days, he is someone I owe a great deal. As an only child I was somewhat of a recluse and when I became a teenager would spend my weekends alone in my greenhouse. Martin made several attempts to make friends with me and simply would not give up. He kept on and eventually we became close friends, spending hours and hours together, often playing darts in each other's bedrooms. The thud of the arrows hitting the board on the back of his door drove his parents potty until one night they cracked and his mum marched into the room with a kitchen mop and literally chased me out of the house. Martin and I also learnt to play backgammon and I can still remember the sweet smell of the tobacco he hid inside the backgammon set and used for his roll-ups.

I was never a roll-up person but at about fourteen started smoking Consulate cigarettes, feeling very smug with myself that the minty flavour would help avoid detection. Menthol cigarettes were all the rage at the time, until word got round that they made you impotent. You've never seen a group of teenagers quit smoking so fast! Together Martin and I had many good childhood adventures, mainly involving his cars. One such adventure ended up bringing the whole of Aix-en-Provence to a halt as he jack-knifed his car and parents' caravan on the main boulevard. On another occasion we managed to send his car into the Grand Union Canal in Watford, closely followed by his dad's car as we tried in vain to use it to tow Martin's out.

Martin and his escapades have always made me laugh and in the days that followed my scandal he was the first person to bring a smile to my face. At the time a whale had swum up the Thames and got stuck. Its life-and-death battle gripped the nation and the headlines began to take the heat off me. Martin's text to me summed it up: 'Thank fuck for the whale.'

Another school buddy, Stuart, and I go back for years. We have never got together without it involving the type of laughter that has you rolling around in agony trying to catch your breath. When I tracked him down by phone he was at Gatwick airport about to catch a flight for a skiing holiday. I quickly garbled: 'Stu, I've got some news. I'm really sorry but—'

'Mate,' he interrupted, 'I'm at the airport and they've got Sky News on and your face is everywhere. I am just trying to convince my mates you're not a total dick.'

Stuart's wife, Karen, is also a long time friend. In fact I introduced them by mistake. I had rather fancied Karen and had planned an evening out with Stuart and another girl. My plans went badly wrong as Stuart and Karen hit it off. In my post-scandal world the pair often joke that Karen had a very lucky escape. Fair point!

By the time I arrived in north Cornwall it was dark and we just had time to collect my sleeping pills from the chemist and then head to Rick Stein's for fish and chips. I could hardly eat a thing and as my phone sprang to life it became clear that the news of my resignation must be breaking on TV. I actually had no idea what was being broadcast. In one of those bizarre twists the television where we were staying literally blew up at about five o'clock during the football results with a flash and smoke billowing out from the back. To this day I have no idea how my nightmare was broadcast and frankly I am glad I never saw those images.

By now it was getting late but I was dreading going to bed. Although I was exhausted and needed rest, I feared the loneliness and solitude that the dark and silence of night would bring. I lay awake thinking of Belinda and the girls. My God, what have I done? How can I have been so stupid? My mind was full of questions. Will I ever see my family again? Where will I live? Will I ever work again? As I gradually felt the sleeping tablets kick in I fell asleep fearing what the day ahead would hold.

Sunday was a long day. Although I woke at seven I felt groggy from the sleeping tablets and unable to eat breakfast for fear of what the general public was reading in the *News of the World*. As we left a rather misty Cornwall my plan was to head for France via a flight from Exeter. We drew into a petrol station and then for the first time I could see the billboards and news headlines. I stayed firmly in my seat but gradually slunk down further and further in case of gazing eyes looking in. As we headed towards Exeter I became more and more troubled by the idea of being on my own in France. I was torn: part of me needed just to run away and escape the whole nightmare, but when I imagined myself alone in France a wave of depression came over me. The isolation would be too much to take! I needed a combination of people and movement to get me through this. Being still in one place or alone was a frightening prospect. In the weeks ahead days became a battle to avoid being alone, or in one place for more than an hour at a time. I took comfort in constant movement from place to place. I've no real idea why. I guess being alone with my thoughts was too raw and my body was still in full-on leadership campaign mode, more used to days on the run than solitary confinement.

I abandoned going to France and as the car drove past Exeter airport I breathed a sigh of relief. In the end I spent the second night in Hampshire in an isolated country house, drugged up with sleeping tablets. The next day word came through that Belinda might be prepared to see me. In the last twenty-four hours she had headed off with the children to Austria with three close friends who'd been able to drop everything at a moment's notice to be with her.

Journalists and photographers were still surrounding our family home and were all over the place trying to track me down. I felt petrified to look out of the window where I was staying. We got in the car again to head for Watford on the Monday morning; I was covered in a hat and glasses to try and disguise myself. Friends had decided that if I was to fly out to Belinda, I could not go alone. I also needed to see my mother to try and reassure her that I was still in one piece. She'd been hounded by the press turning up at her house. Even my father in his mid-eighties was tracked down in Italy and the press turned up at his flat in the outskirts of the university city of Padua. I'd not even had a chance to talk to him about what was going on before some Italian tabloid contact was buzzing at his door. It was a similar picture with three of Belinda's sisters, one of whom was tracked down in Denmark, another in France, and Caroline, her eldest sister, facing the press on the doorstep at the family farm. All were offered large sums of money in return for revealing family details. Even the local vicar was under pressure to reveal details of our marriage certificate.

Back in Watford my mother had told me that the coast was clear at her house, but I was still anxious the press might be there. As we drove closer and closer it seemed we'd not been followed, but to be safe we drove away from my mother's house to a side road so I could avoid being directly in front of the house. As I stepped out of the car this guy jumped out of the bushes and ran after me and I had to leg it to get to see my mum. There was hardly time for a hug! We knew that the journalist would quickly spread the word that I was in Watford and the house would be surrounded very soon. I told my mum to pack some clothes and that we would have to leave within ten minutes. As we left the house my mate created a diversion and the journalist followed his car. Mum and I headed off not knowing where we were going as I hit the phone to try and find a safe house to allow us time to plan what to do. I called my old friend Mickey and he immediately said to come round. It was a great comfort to give him a hug and chat for a few moments and say how sorry I was for everything. From his house we managed to book flights to Munich leaving in a few hours' time. I knew this was not too far from the ski resort where Belinda and the children were. Even if she refused to see me I felt better knowing I was getting closer. As we drove to Heathrow word came out that the airport photographers were on the look-out for me. In the end we managed to make it to the gate without event other than countless fellow passengers glancing across trying to figure out where they'd seen my face. The answer was on every national newspaper that day.

The Monday press had been full of my scandal. *The Daily Telegraph* covered the whole front page with a photo and the headline 'How could he?' – and to my horror this was the complimentary paper on the plane. As I slumped as low as I could get in my seat everybody around me was staring at my photo and reading the story. In the row of seats on my left I overheard two passengers:

'My God, he was married and had two children.'

'It's awful, what a mess that party is in.'

I wanted to get off the plane, run, move, do anything other than be strapped in for two hours with more and more eyes glancing in my direction. It was unbearable. My mind could not focus on reading or music, I just reread the sick bag over and over and did my best to hide under a baseball cap and pray for the 'cabin crew, ten minutes to landing' announcement.

Screwing Up

We hired a car and headed off in the direction of the ski resort, Bad Gastein, but my patience was quickly tested as we began to get lost in the outskirts of Munich with a German-speaking satnav system. After several *links* and a few *rechts* we ended up down a dead end road. My mother managed to lose her glasses under her seat and I managed to drop the satnav under mine as I was trying to switch it into English. We were lost, hungry, tired and facing the prospect of trying to track down Belinda in the middle of nowhere – not a great moment! Thankfully the directions got easier and by the next morning I was desperate to visit Belinda in her hotel. It was now four days since I'd bolted over the garden fence and I had no idea how she would react when she saw me. She was calm and cold but allowed me to talk to the children, who were full of skiing adventures and thankfully seemed pleased to see me. We agreed to meet later this time to go skiing. I was absolutely frozen, having just travelled in what I was wearing, so my mum and I went in search of warmer clothes and kitted ourselves out for the minus-eight conditions. Belinda has always loved skiing whilst I've been a bit reluctant. I find there is just too much stuff involved. I struggle to juggle gloves, skis, hat, poles and pass and usually end up dropping and losing things. I get too hot then too cold. I hate getting on the lifts and then I am too scared to actually ski and keep falling over. Give me a nice book and a swimming pool any day! Apart from not really enjoying the experience there is another problem – I just can't ski. So Belinda's invitation to meet up the side of a mountain presented a dilemma: risk death on the white stuff, or risk not seeing my wife. When I found her she simply headed off down a red run and I had no option but to plunge off the ski lift and follow.

Making it down the slopes in Austria was a turning point in all sorts of ways. I actually enjoyed the experience of skiing as the two of us swept along a straight piece of piste flanked by pine trees covered in white and with the sun blasting down. I was baking hot in the ski gear but buzzing along and concentrating so hard that for the first time in a few days my mind felt unburdened. I found myself laughing out loud, Belinda smiled, we touched; could the impossible happen – could we really survive this ordeal?

Gradually the late winter sky darkened and we found ourselves running out of time to get down the mountain. The lifts were now well and truly closed and the only way down was on the two thin things strapped to my feet. Perhaps after all Belinda's laughter was cover for a cunning plot to leave me with a broken neck in some tragic ski mishap. The rather pleasant snowy path now turned into a sheer drop that left me feeling slightly wobbly when I looked down. You know that sensation you get when you look over a cliff or the top of the Empire State Building – you feel a bit dizzy. Anyway all of that kicked in and after a few failed attempts I followed Belinda down on my bottom skidding slowly from side to side and arriving at the base wet, worn out and worried again. My undignified descent was hardly in keeping with the new more macho image I was keen to present. Belinda was cool with it, though, and we agreed to meet again the next day. It was an important step or slide in the right direction. I went to bed hopeful and swallowed my Prozac and sleeping tablets actually looking forward to the morning.

The next few days were unreal. Away from the reality of home and headlines I began to rebuild my relationship with Belinda and the girls. My mother returned to England and we all agreed it would be safe if I stayed on. We were panicky when a strange car pulled up near us or a camera flash went off but despite endless attempts the press just didn't catch on to a remote resort in Austria. Eventually all this had to come to an end and I knew I had to get back to England and face the music. I'll never forget leaving the hotel; I could hardly drive the car for tears and sobbed all the way to Munich, only interrupted by the bloody German satnav telling me to go *geradeaus* every ten minutes.

With my woolly hat and skiing jacket I hoped to sneak into Heathrow unnoticed. Olly and Owen were ready and waiting and just as I came into arrivals the Olympic medallist Denise Lewis arrived to a round of flashbulbs, creating the perfect distraction. I quickly darted behind her and found Owen, who was not impressed with my disguise.

'You look like a sex offender.'

'Great, let's just get out of here.'

In the end the photographers won and the next day the tabloids had me pictured unshaven, with silly hat and coat – and, yes, Owen's description was not far off the mark. At least now I was in the care of Owen and Olly, two close work colleagues and mates who I trusted completely. I was desperate to try and get home to pick up fresh clothes and my new credit card and PIN, as all my cards had been cancelled when my wallet was stolen a few days before I resigned.

Despite the danger of lurking press we managed to sneak into the house for ten minutes and I did a *Supermarket Sweep*-style dash around to collect post and clothes and set the answering machine. We then took a gamble and stayed the night in the village with my close friends Chris and Alison Day. As we found spare rooms to crash in the press were just a few hundred yards away. And so I spent the next few days in a pink bed surrounded by dolls, as the Days' daughter had given up her bedroom. It's a kind of friendship and support that you can't imagine getting when something like this hits. As two million people read about my exploits there was a real life left in tatters and it was only thanks to the kindness of people like Alison and Chris that I survived. They did not question me; they gave unconditional friendship and safe haven even though it caused difficult questions from the kids and lying to neighbours and friends to deny knowledge of my whereabouts. I will never forget what they did for me or the support of another set of friends who helped in the early days but whose friendship sadly could not in the end survive the ordeal.

It was now almost a full week since the *News of the World* had appeared. As the next Sunday approached we were told that a follow-up story was planned. On the Friday, Owen and the Lib Dems' head of press, Mark Littlewood, went to a meeting with the *News of the World* to discuss what they planned next and the possibility of some kind of deal with them. In essence if I agreed to a full and frank interview they would stop running the story. After much debate we decided against any interview and to let them print what they wanted instead. Saturday was drawn out as we waited to see what they would publish next.

I was desperate to be distracted so decided to head for Watford and Vicarage Road to see my team play. I've supported my home side for years but found the pressure of work and living in Winchester made it hard to get to games. I'd been asked to go officially into the directors' box on one occasion but hated it. I turned up without a tie and was made to borrow one, I wanted to watch the pre-match build-up but had to make polite conversation and, worst of all, I wanted to jump up when we scored but had to stay in my seat under a blanket and clap enthusiastically. All too stuffy for a real fan. I much prefer going with Mickey and his son into the stands.

Covered in about ten layers of hats, gloves and jumpers I was pretty confident I would be protected from the freezing January weather and anybody who might recognise the latest scandal-hit MP. We managed to win 4-0, which lifted my mood a little as we waited for the first editions of the Sunday papers to hit central London at around 11 p.m. After the match, to kill time, Owen and I headed off to eat in Wandsworth and found a restaurant, Louvaine, on St John's Hill. There were a few glances as we took a table hidden in a corner and we settled down for what we hoped would be an anonymous meal. About half-way through the evening I managed to blow my cover spectacularly. Owen had gone to the loo, leaving me with strict instructions to do nothing other than eat. When he returned he found me surrounded by several waitresses trying to put out a small fire I'd managed to start by fiddling with my napkin and the candle. As the flames leaped up from the table every one of our fellow diners' attention was on me, in total contrast to Owen's planned strategy. When we eventually picked up the first edition of the *News of the World* there was nothing particularly new. At last I felt we might be reaching the beginning of the end. But I also knew I couldn't keep on hiding so the following week it was decided I should get back to work.

I was petrified as I drove into the entrance of Parliament to vote on a key piece of terrorism legislation. I wanted to hide in my office, but voting requires your physical presence as you file down a corridor just outside the chamber, pushing and shoving with colleagues. My nerves were soon calmed as a string of MPs from all parties came up to pat me on the back, shake hands and tell me to keep my spirits up. It was worth the effort, as the government lost by one vote – thank God I made it.

Getting back to work in Winchester was just as daunting. I had a surgery planned in the village of Swanmore, which we decided to go ahead with. It was fully booked but as I drew up I had no idea if anybody would arrive for their appointments. My sense of dread grew when I arrived to find the village hall surrounded by cameras, photographers and live satellite TV trucks. Sleepy Swanmore had never seen anything like it before. The local BBC chap, Peter Henley, asked me how I could possibly carry on as an MP with all this media attention going on. Bloody hell – it was his camera crew blocking the entrance to my surgery, making it a frightening experience for my constituents to see me. If nobody turned up the press would have their next headline. I waited behind my desk in the hall until, thankfully, the first appointment turned up, then the second and the third. In fact they all came, they discussed their problems and I was close to tears as they all urged me to carry on with my job and ignore the press. It was another turning point and began to restore my faith in human nature.

Throughout this period our house in the quiet village of Bramdean was under siege from a combination of journalists and photographers. Eventually the number dwindled to a bunch of freelance snappers hoping to get a shot and sell it on, but in the days after the story broke anyone turning up at the house was news. As various friends and family checked post whilst we were away, the press felt the need to report the smallest detail. A close friend of ours, Clare, let herself in to get some things for Belinda. This made the local TV news, which confidently reported, much to Clare's amusement, that she was our cleaner. Even our poor builders, who were coming to the end of constructing an extension, were exposed to a media onslaught, but of course what all the press wanted was the first snap of Belinda and me. In the weeks that followed they turned up everywhere – at the airport when I returned from Austria, at my London flat and then literally jumping out of woods as Belinda and I walked our springer spaniel, Coco, and tried to find time to talk.

By the time we did both move back home I'd hoped things would have calmed down, but instead they just moved to a new stage. Now we had nice letters pushed through the door as the press attempted to get the first interview with Belinda. It was pathetic! The letters all started with expressions of sympathy, saying how brave Belinda was; some even said it was awful to be put in the media spotlight, despite those very papers continuing to print stories. As they failed to get any interviews they just started to make up half-page articles with sets of paragraphs speculating on our future. A classic technique was to quote what 'sources around Westminster' said, when in reality the source would just be another journalist. This went on for weeks and as Belinda remained silent it seemed to fuel rather than silence things.

The more Belinda declined the more desperate the papers became and then they started offering money until in the end a tabloid bid over £100,000 to get her side of the story. Although she turned down this offer Belinda wanted to end the speculation and was also determined not to appear like some kind of loyal political wife shutting up for the good of the party. She was furious and certainly not in the mood to take some of the bitchy rubbish being written at the time without putting her side. The likes of Ann Widdecombe, Carol Malone and Ulrika Jonsson had all rushed into print with a load of patronising words of wisdom for Belinda – most instructing her to leave me. In the end she decided the only way to shut them up and move on was to agree to an interview. Owen, my researcher, gets on with Belinda and together they looked at the options.

In the next village lived an acquaintance of ours who worked for *Hello!* magazine. They'd made contact and Belinda felt very comfortable doing an interview with their journalist just a few farms away from our house. They paid a fee which Belinda accepted and although it was much less than others were offering, *Hello!* felt like a softer way to speak out. Of course, when the article came out all the tabloids that had been asking for an interview were quick to attack her for speaking out. You soon learn in a situation like this that you're damned if you do or damned if you don't.

Now that Belinda was on the record, talk turned to when I would say something. This was tricky as I was in no place to really understand what was going on in my head and I was aware that the party wanted me to disappear as soon as possible.

I decided to speak to my local paper first. The *Hampshire Chronicle* is as non-tabloid as you can get; it's not that long since the whole front page was taken up with adverts selling logs, a litter of gundogs and second-hand horse boxes. So my scandal was the biggest story they'd had since the Romans left town. I wasn't really ready to talk to anyone, but radio silence had to be broken. I just about got through the hour-long ordeal and the paper printed a very fair front page.

About a month later I wanted to do a more reflective piece and agreed to pen 10,000 words for the *Sunday Times* Review section. I wanted it to be as frank as possible and spoke about how tough I found getting older, a symbol of which was the very public loss of my hair. By Monday morning all the nationals interpreted this as 'Oaten blames sex on baldness', or punchier versions of that. I was made to look ridiculous as the lobby journalists collectively took the piss! I was torn between just going back into hiding or trying to explain and communicate. Yes, I had screwed up and hurt my family, but I felt a need to try and talk about it.

The press called every day wanting stories. I needed to feed them every month to get them off my back, but also for my own progress, to keep busy. The decision to talk was not popular with colleagues. John Barrett, a blunt Scottish MP, came up to me in the Commons all smiles and said: 'Mark, you do realise you're making a fool of yourself and damaging all of us, why don't you just shut up?' I understand why he said it and I felt awful about the damage my affair had caused the party and my fellow Lib Dem MPs but his comments hurt for weeks. He had no idea how hard it was to deal with this situation. Each day I had press cuttings on my computer and the story just would not go away. By now my name had become shorthand for scandal and disgust, to be used freely by diary columnists and writers. Jeremy Clarkson said he 'would rather climb into Mark Oaten than the new Ford Focus', which was at least funny, but Richard Littlejohn seemed obsessed with me, using any chance to describe me as a nasty lowlife. He painted the picture of an evil, sick monster – I was mortified. It was relentless; I'd never had such abuse thrown at me and I would sit in front of my computer close to tears as these columnists tore me to pieces. I would shout back: 'Look, I'm not like that – you don't even know me.' I felt powerless to respond because, of course, it was my bloody fault in the first place, but even if I did want to respond there was no point. Who would have any sympathy?

It was against this climate that I agreed to present a ten-minute film for *Newsnight* to try and examine what it was like to face this kind of media onslaught. I interviewed a shrink in the Freud Museum, a tabloid editor and Michael Brown, the journalist and former Tory MP who was caught up in the Tory 'back to basics' media wave when he announced he was gay. In its own strange way it gave me a chance to reflect and realise that my fall from grace was not an isolated experience. Talking to Michael made me see that there was life after scandal and keeping busy with a camera crew was a welcome distraction.

Interestingly, the one bit of press that seemed to be welcomed by many was the only joint interview Belinda and I agreed to give. We were interviewed by Martha Kearney for *Woman's Hour* and it resulted in some really nice letters.

Worse even than the media, however, were the millions of words written on websites. My downfall was one of the first political scandals in the blog era. Within seconds of the story breaking bloggers were having a ball with jokes and theories about what I'd done. It took weeks before I could read any of it and much of it would have resulted in legal action if it had appeared in a newspaper, but the web operates fast, free and cruelly. Years on I've yet to see a single blog or comment on the internet that is an accurate account of what took place. Most just keep repeating the same lurid suggestions about me and of course as time passes they become the truth, repeated as a factual history of what I did. If it was not so hurtful it would be rather amusing that hundreds of bloggers and a fair few newspaper columnists seem so happy to print these comments with such confidence.

As the weeks went by I started to get out and about. Around Winchester people would come up in the street, give me a hug, smile, offer words of encouragement. Typical was 'you're a bloody idiot – but you're a good MP and that's what counts'. It was overwhelming and gave me so much help to find some sense of confidence. Despite that the mere act of walking anywhere was dreadful. People would stare at me all the time. I can't find the words to explain what this feels like. If you've won an Olympic gold I'm sure the attention is weird but wonderful, but all I could think about was the awful thoughts people might be having about me. I developed a walk which never allowed my eyes to leave the floor and I started to become hunched up and look hunted. I also lost weight and went down in shirt and trouser size as I lost my appetite and forced down what little food I could stomach. As I shuffled around avoiding eye contact my confidence and appearance were at rock bottom.

Facing family and friends was yet more terrifying. I was dreading the first school run. Our children went to a wonderful, picturesque, well-run village school in Cheriton. Everybody chats in the playground and Belinda and I had made so many friends through the school. We've never had political friends, like so many MPs; instead fellow parents and neighbours have formed a key part of our social life. As I drove up and dropped Alice and Milly at the school gates I was unsure how the other children and parents would react. As we walked past the post office an elderly gentleman, who I'm sure gets the *Telegraph* each day, looked up. Damn, I thought – of all the people to bump into! 'Young man,' he said, 'let me tell you this – you just jolly well hold your head up.' I could have burst into tears. There was a similar response from the local school community.

To this day, I've only had a couple of episodes where people have shouted anything unkind. It has taught me that I am lucky to have such wonderful friends and constituents – but that there is such a mismatch between what the diary and gossip writers say and how the public think.

After three weeks living from a suitcase and moving from location to location I was desperate to get back home. By now Belinda and the girls were home and we wanted to try and recreate a normal environment for the children. Of course things were far from normal. I slept in the downstairs bedroom and slowly we rebuilt a family structure. Part of this process meant Belinda and I needed our time to talk, fight, argue and make up. Belinda's mood would swing from blind rage to a tenderness towards me. When she was angry she really went for it on some occasions, lashing out and hitting me. It was alarming and it hurt, but she needed to get it out of her system and I needed to take the blows and, apart from a broken finger, I never came to much harm. Two months later, Belinda spoke about hitting me in a magazine interview, which prompted the chief constable of Hampshire Police to write to me and ask if I wanted to take action against her! I guess they have to follow up every lead but this was ridiculous.

Trying to find time to talk and be alone was tough. Our house was still subject to the occasional freelance photographer and they would lurk around the village waiting to catch us. As we went on walks in the surrounding countryside photographers would appear amongst the trees and undergrowth. In the end we would just wave at them or take a stupid pleasure from giving them the slip – but their presence was a constant reminder of what I'd done. The real fear we had was how to protect the children from photographers. As we left the house we would scan the village hall trying not to let the girls see how worried we were.

As the media storm calmed down I was left with hundreds of questions from colleagues, family and friends, keen to know what was really behind the *News of the World* story. For them there were two questions. Just what had I done and why?

I have never actually sat and read the papers, but of course I have seen the transcripts and endless dissecting of it on the internet. The basic *News of the World* story is true, but in other papers and websites some of the language used and the speculation and assumptions about what I did are unbelievable and hurtful. I have never felt it was right to challenge, or threaten legal action, because at the end of the day I screwed up. There is, however, a real concern about the lack of control over websites. Some even accused me of being a paedophile, but there is no real power to challenge this, or some of the other bizarre rumours.

It's hard to even begin to understand what led a happily married man to see a male escort. At around that time I had been working crazy hours and was on a treadmill of meetings, interviews and speeches. Although each day was interesting and different they actually blurred into the same routine of pumping myself up with adrenalin to fight the general exhaustion. Jumping from one reception, or event, to another, I began to get into the habit of knocking back a few glasses at each. By the end of the evening a combination of tiredness and alcohol would help me sleep, but also made me fairly emotional.

Screwing Up

It was on such a night that I sought out the number of an escort in the back of a magazine and went to his flat in south London. I know it's hard to believe but when I was there I did not feel guilt, or panic and the guy actually made me feel like this was the most normal thing in the world. He was polite, friendly, businesslike and in total control, giving me no sense that I was exploiting him. He was good looking and I was certainly envious of his youthfulness. We never had intercourse and I stayed for less than an hour, and then I remember collapsing back at my flat in a state of exhaustion, drunkenness, guilt and confusion. I had been fascinated by the experience and although I knew it was wrong I wanted to explore more. I carried on seeing him; each time I visited it was late at night and on an evening when I would be staying in London.

Around the beginning of March 2005 the political world was heating up as the general election campaign was about to start. My life became even more frantic and I was away from London campaigning and jumping in and out of TV studios several times a day. The next time I saw the escort was when the *News of the World* journalist showed me his picture that awful morning almost a year later. To this day I don't feel angry with him selling his story. This was entirely my fault, no point blaming anybody else.

But the real question about all of this is not what I did but why. I wish there was a simple answer. My sexuality had never been something I ever had reason to question. As a teenager I was as keen as all my mates to get a girlfriend and quickly had a whole string of relationships. It was all perfectly normal although I did have relations with a couple of married women in my early twenties. By the time I married Belinda in 1992 I had fallen head over heels in love with her and our relationship was wonderful.

So how did the need to experiment with my sexuality start? In months of counselling after the affair became public I spent hours going through the reasons. I think there are a number of complex factors at work.

Seeing this 23-year-old man was obviously an enormous personal risk. I used my own phone to call him and made no attempt to hide the number. I turned up in my work clothes, on one occasion direct from a television studio. Yet I had no real concept of the risk I was taking. I didn't think for a moment that he would have a clue who I was. I never made much of a calculation over this, but just assumed that he was unlikely to watch *Newsnight* and that I wasn't a well-known public figure. In fact if I'd been thinking rationally I would have realised that by 2004 my face was in fact in the national news most weeks and the various major home affairs issues were raising my profile to a level I'd not experienced before. But I was not thinking rationally and even though others may have seen me as a politician, or a public face, for my part I felt very unknown and anonymous. People would stop and point in the street, or come up and make a comment about something I'd said, or done, but frankly I was a fringe player and I still find it hard to believe that I was well known enough to be recognised.

It's been suggested to me since that I did really know the risks I was taking and that this was a motivation, firstly because the danger of being caught added to the excitement and secondly that I was so fed up with work that I wanted to be caught to bring things to an end. In long conversations with my shrink I've explored both these views. At no time did I consciously think 'Wow, how exciting, what a risk' or 'Let's hope tomorrow I get caught and have to resign.' These thoughts never entered my head so we're dealing with a sub-conscious motivation that I'm now asked to understand. I simply don't get the link, however hard I try to make one. I was depressed and stressed at work, but there were surely plenty of other ways to have given that up other than create a scandal?

That said, I do understand the danger argument. After all each week hundreds of people commit adultery and part of the buzz is the risk and feeling of naughtiness. Some people get their excitement from danger, say from bungee jumping, or motorbikes, others take drugs, or drink too much. I guess we all need a thrill from something.

There's another important issue for me over this kind of affair. This was not a case of a husband carrying on a secret affair for months and falling in love with somebody else. In my case there were no hidden texts, letters, secret meetings or presents. It was emotionless and whilst it was unforgivable, in my view Belinda could at least gain some comfort that I was not some businessman who'd run off with his secretary after a long affair. I also think that in some strange way Belinda took some comfort that my unfaithfulness was with a man, not a woman. It may have been a tremendous initial shock, but the lack of emotion involved and sense in which there was not a woman to compete with have helped us both move forward.

So why then did I take this risk with a man, not a woman? It is the six million dollar question. As I've said before it would be easy to suddenly declare that I am gay and have been suppressed for years. People, and I totally understand why, like to have tidy explanations and are suspicious of doubt, or unclear answers. If I was at the dispatch box at Westminster my explanation would be shouted down in seconds! I now understand that risk and danger did play a small part, but the motivation for taking that risk with a man comes from deeper sexual doubts and issues about both my childhood and ageing process.

I don't think that on the sexuality line many people can be 100 per cent gay or 100 per cent heterosexual. I am certainly not, and at times in thier lives some people experiment along the spectrum. There is, particularly amongst the younger generation, a less firm set of rules and boundaries. A few years ago the word 'metrosexual' was coined to describe a more youthful urban male who was happy to cook, buy moisturiser and watch football. Whilst he felt straight in his sexuality, he'd have lots of gay friends and feel easy about the idea of same-sex relationships, perhaps even wishing to experiment with them himself. I am not sure that I've described 'metrosexual' that well, but I felt that, out of those awful labels we have to be given, it was the one that summed up my own feeling about myself.

I am just not the six-foot, rugby-playing, beer-drinking farmer that enjoys lads' weekends and thinks a woman's place is in the kitchen. I'm not comfortable with that extreme blokey image and have often felt awkward mixing in that type of world. I don't easily fit into that culture and have always found it much easier to chat to women at supper parties than men. I am a bit of a drip when it comes to crying and even drizzle when somebody is evicted from *The X Factor*, much to the amusement of the whole family. The idea of a weekend-long stag party fills me with dread and I can struggle to do laddish chat. So does that mean I am gay? No, but it means I completely at ease with those that are and have found chatting to gay work colleagues fun as they are less hung up on the macho stuff, and have been envious of the rather happy-go-lucky approach they seem to have to life in general. There is also something interesting about the world they live in. It feels very free, without responsibility and certainly energetic and young. I am sure I am dealing in stereotypes here, but to an outsider looking in there is a certain fascination. But perhaps, above all, and here I think lies a big clue in my case, there is a youthfulness about it. It is in total contrast to the life of the forty-something Hampshire dad, married with two children, who is getting fat and losing his looks. I think I am driven by an attempt to escape middle age and recapture my youth. I have no problem admitting that I can look at a guy and think he is good looking, then again I find women attractive. Talking to mates it's common to be able to admire other people's looks but for me there is nearly always a slight hint of envy thrown in.

I wish I understood why youth is so important to me. After all we all get old, and I should just live with it! But I keep wanting to fight against it and certainly feel that I was driven to experimenting or trying to recapture my youth. The doubts about sexuality and search for youthfulness are part of my DNA, but in working out all these issues with my counsellor other issues have emerged, in particular my childhood. This sounds too much like a shrink-and-client couch scene to be true. 'Tell me about your childhood' are the opening words of any number of sketches, but it's true – they do ask that. In my case I'd given it very little thought, but when I was asked about my first sexual experience a flood of memories came back.

Before I talk about what happened, I should say that I remain very doubtful that any of this explains my actions. I can't remember a great deal about what took place and have boxed the whole thing away for years to such an extent that it was only during post-scandal counselling that the issue came up. It was when I was about nine or ten and involved a two-year period when I was regularly asked to sexually massage a man much older than me. He was unknown to my parents but in a position of trust. It felt totally normal and I certainly never felt abused. Clearly it was wrong, but it happened and I've not even been that worried about it. Belinda knew, and now so do however many people bother to read this book. I tell it not for sympathy and not to explain or excuse what I did, because I don't get the connection. It is, however, part of me and I have to listen to the professionals that tell me it must have played its role. If telling this results in headlines that I blame my actions on childhood abuse then that is wrong. I don't blame it, I have never felt abused, hold no grudge and do not wish to drag the case up today. It was, however, something that should not have happened and I guess my head at least tells me that all these years later my sexuality may have been affected by my first sexual experience. In saying this I don't for one moment belittle those that have suffered from abuse. I think it is right that the law is tough in this area and victims are given full support if they wish to take legal action, even years later.

So there are numerous messy issues flying around in my life and I had no idea during the winter of 2004–5 that my actions would ever become public, or that I would have to sit down and try to figure out what I was doing. Life's not simple, the answers are not easy, but a combination of sexual experimentation, danger seeking, hunger for youth and childhood memories seem to have combined to make me how I am.

Blaming it on one event or calling it a mid-life crisis would be simple – but wrong. Of course not everybody runs off to have an affair when they turn forty. It's more readily acceptable to fork out on a Harley-Davidson and spend weekends fiddling around getting oil on the garage floor. For the less daring, there are basically two options. Do you fight turning forty, with a sudden interest in Radio 1, iPods and Converse trainers? Or do you just give in to your ageing life, rent an allotment and play Duran Duran tapes on a worn-out Walkman?

I think I ended up somewhere in the middle. I started listening to classical music on my iPod, but went to see The Feeling live in concert. I went to Paris and Amsterdam with just a rucksack but stayed in a four-star hotel. I started buying the *Telegraph* but loved watching *Big Brother*. I went on a twelve-week wine course but still buy the £3.99 plonk. I am just a walking contradiction but at least I discovered that I am not alone.

After my scandal I received literally thousands of emails and letters from forty-year-old men with similar stories to tell. Many of them admitted to affairs, which in some cases were still going on. I found it extraordinary that total strangers would write to me with such explicit details about their sex lives, which they obviously sought to keep so private at home. Most letters started with sympathy for my situation and then went on to detail, sometimes rather graphically, what they were doing. There were a few rather worrying offers of 'friendship', and one guy offered his assistance as my butler, happy to help arrange my 'various homes' in return for companionship. Others said they had always fancied me and an alarming number asked for a signed picture. On the whole most had a story to tell and a familiar pattern emerged. A bad childhood experience, a happy marriage, children and then an office fling, or visits to prostitutes which they could not stop. I had the very strong sense that most were unhappy at leading this double life but found it hard to give it up.

Others had been through a bad spell but encouraged me that things can get back to normal. I didn't really have time to take all this in as I was in the eye of the storm but months later I found many of the messages a real comfort. Although unlike me these forty-year-olds have been able to deal with their demons in private.

My public ordeal allowed the media to speculate and write about the idea of a mid-life crisis yet again. When something like this happens it needs a label – some kind of short-cut description that people can use: 'Oh, he's had a nervous breakdown or a mid-life crisis.' Sweeping statements don't come near to explaining the complex set of circumstances that lead individuals to go off the rails, but the concept of crisis in mid-life is something I have become fascinated by. Forty is a mid-way point in life, if you assume you'll be lucky enough to make it to eighty. But it's not just the age itself: forty is also the point at which you're no longer the young Turk at work, when parents start to get elderly and when children start to grow up. The financial commitments are often at their scariest: paying for a growing family and perhaps tuition fees and care home fees. It's also a point of no return. If you want a career change then time is running out before you're too old to move. All this comes just when many women's sex drive increases whilst at the same time men's might be slowing down. The trigger for a crisis can lie in a combination of these experiences but typically the death of a parent or losing a job will lead to many men reflecting on what they have achieved to date and what's left to look forward to.

This year a million people in the UK will hit forty. They will get the cheesy cards, the pressure for a party and jokes about being past it. Many will have a great time and not think twice about it but many will also look at the greying hair, bags under the eyes, and increasing aches and pains.

Beyond the tabloid headlines I found some well-written and informative articles about the whole experience. Philip Hodson, a fellow of the British Association of Psychotherapy, wrote a piece on sexual self-destruction in the *Independent* which I could relate to. It said:

> As men enter their mid-life zone, with waning testosterone levels and more fragile sexual responses, they tend to seek out increasingly extreme sexual experiences. There's even a repeated association between experimenting with a first or a renewal of a homosexual experience after the death of a man's father … There is the role of the unconscious mind in these destructive unmaskings. For many husbands, particularly in middle age, there is a quiet unexplained desperation to escape a pattern of life. Perhaps their career no longer fits them but they cannot easily think of shedding off its constricting skin. Part of them wants to play, part seeks attention, part wants to drop out, part wants to be young again, part wants to be mothered, part wants to be an artist but none of these is considered rational. Instead they get themselves into a horrible public pickle, rather like the ex-Director of Public Prosecutions, Sir Alan Green, who of all people was caught kerb-crawling in the early 1990s, or Hugh Grant, who invited a hooker into his car – or like Mark Oaten. Their tragedy is that secretly they must have wanted to be caught.

Now, for me, reading this and other pieces like it was on one level very powerful as columnist after columnist sought to explain my actions, but on another level just imagine what it is like to have everybody examining you in this way. It was as if the entire media was a shrink and I was permanently on the couch as the weeks passed by.

By the summer of 2006 I was left trying to figure all this out in my head and at the same time I was still being followed by photographers, stared at when I went out and torn apart by the gossip columnists. I could just about deal with that but my real battle was just about to start. I had to start fighting to save my marriage, my career, my health and my future.

10

Not so Honourable Members

Spring 2009 was one of the darkest times to be a member of Parliament. The *Daily Telegraph* had purchased a disk which included all our expenses claims and receipts for a four-year period. In dramatic fashion they moved from party to party revealing the worst cases day by day for over a month.

The atmosphere around Westminster was a mixture of fear and panic. Fear that you'd be next, as MPs nervously glanced at missed calls on mobiles, praying they were not from the *Telegraph* team; panic as members agreed to pay back amounts and the three party leaders went into a bidding war to see who could introduce the toughest measures to clamp down on abuse. Normally such statements of apology and action would draw a line under the story, but this time politicians were powerless to stop events and every attempt to move the story on failed. I'd never experienced anything like it – all the normal rules of media management were torn up and for over a month the *Daily Telegraph* set the agenda, virtually deciding who should resign as MPs dropped like flies.

Everywhere you turned Honourable Members would be in huddles discussing the scandal. The latest victim would walk down corridors receiving sympathetic pats on the back or awkward glances. In my conversations with colleagues several broke down in tears and I became convinced that somebody might even commit suicide as the pressure grew and grew. There was a mixture of anger and frustration as MPs watched events spiralling out of control. Like everybody else I was worried about my own expenses – would they stand up to public scrutiny? My total claims were high and often near the maximum allowed. The combination of a large mortgage on my flat in London, a high office rent in Winchester and always employing my full quota of staff put me in the top quarter of spenders. I'd not gone mad on luxury items, never using the so-called John Lewis list – I was more at the Ikea end of the range. Although I was anxious at what the *Telegraph* would do, I felt slightly more prepared than many others. In 2005 I heard that a freelance journalist had put in a Freedom of Information request on my expenses claims along with fourteen other MPs including Tony Blair, Gordon Brown, Michael Howard and Charles Kennedy. The case dragged on for ages as the Speaker kept challenging the request for publication, something I was never consulted on! In the end, after court rulings, the Commons authorities were forced to publish and I found one year's worth of claims splashed over the press. They made great fun of a bunk bed and a £5 pair of oven gloves. Ironically, because I had put in receipts for items under £250 I'd drawn attention to myself. (You try and be open by itemising your oven gloves and you still get burnt!) This had all happened a year before the *Telegraph* exclusive and seemed to pass after a 24-hour frenzy. A year later it was a bigger story but this time I was not the focus and thankfully only got a small mention over two irons I had purchased.

My expenses weren't in the same league as duck houses, flipping homes or paying for gardeners but I still felt awkward about justifying my items. My constituents seemed reasonably reassured and I got just four emails on the subject, one actually pointing out I'd failed to claim for council tax when I could have! The local press was mildly irritating – in particular the *Portsmouth News* became obsessed with a bath I had fitted when my London flat flooded. I'd had to rip out the bathroom after three floods and although I only claimed for the essential work a new bath appeared on the main builder's receipt. It was a standard cheap plastic bath, but unfortunately its brand name was Whirlpool, which convinced the paper

I'd ordered an all-singing, all-dancing Jacuzzi. Far from it but the episode showed how sensitive the expenses saga was.

Now with hindsight I can see why buying beds with public money looks bad. But at the time you're told you can have a flat in London, you're told you can furnish it and that's what you do – it's part of the system and part of what you're allowed. At first when you get elected and the allowances are explained it's all a blur. Bit by bit the Fees Office explains what you can do and soon claiming for this and that becomes the culture. It's as if you're entitled to it, so why not claim it?

In the end the *Telegraph* claimed the jobs of the Community Secretary, Hazel Blears, and the Home Secretary, Jacqui Smith, and many backbenchers were forced to announce they were standing down at the next election. I felt for colleagues caught up in the scandal, in particular those that had faced a public trial by media, such as Julie Kirkbride, who was subject to a relentless campaign against her from the local media and constituents. In many ways it was a witch hunt and, whatever the rights and wrongs of her expenses, it was no way to resolve the issue. I gave her a hug when she next appeared in the Commons and I make no apology for trying to be kind to MPs who see their career end this way. We now face over a hundred MPs standing down at the election with somewhat shaky prospects for future employment, as either individually or collectively we are all damaged by the scandal.

There is no-one as 'ex' as an ex-MP and that's never going to be truer than after the expenses row or in my case after a scandal. The track record of former MPs in finding jobs is patchy to say the least. At worst some end up never working again, relying on benefits or leaving the country. Sue Doughty, the former member for Guildford, recalls how she ended up at the very job centre she'd opened just a year before. Others, unable to find an employer to take them on, turn to self-employment as media or speaking consultants, or they may set up their own business, like Harvey Proctor, the Tory MP who quit following a sex scandal in the 1980s and went on to open a shirt shop in Richmond.

These days a CV bearing the words 'member of Parliament' is about as welcome as an application from King Herod to run a crèche. Look beyond the negative image, though, and you'll find MPs with plenty of skills, contacts, energy and ability. The problem is that so few people really understand the experiences we can bring to running businesses, charities and public services. I find it slightly ironic that when you're an MP these organisations seek your help, advice and knowledge but don't then recognise and exploit those very same skills at a later date. I am realistic enough to know that in some ways my time as a member of Parliament has made me less employable even though I am far more skilled and experienced now than when I was MD of a public relations consultancy. Some of the headhunters are only interested in what I did before I was elected, disregarding the last thirteen years as something to be hidden or explained away. I hope I have worked hard enough in the last few years to address all of this and I've recently found it encouraging to join six boards as a trustee or non-executive director. I will also never forget the faith that Ray Hodgkinson and the British Healthcare Trades Association showed in me by keeping me as a director after my scandal. I've been offered some full-time jobs too, but to date have decided against quitting Parliament early and plan to hang on to the end. It will, however, be a crowded end with 200 or so CVs flying around with the initials 'MP' on them after the next election.

The biggest expenses scandal scalp of them all belonged to the Speaker himself. I thought that Michael Martin was turned into a scapegoat by MPs. Whilst he stood as a symbol of the old regime, too many MPs were very quick to suddenly become advocates of change when they'd been more happy to support the old guard and institutions represented by the Speaker. He was a kindly Speaker, torn between trying to protect MPs and moving with the times. In the end he did neither. The day he announced his resignation we all rushed into the chamber, like a crowd gathering for a public execution. As Martin processed into the Commons, loyal MPs formed a line of honour as he passed through the Members' Lobby, just feet from the chamber itself. There was a outbreak of applause and tears, adding to the very human tragedy of it all.

Of course as politicians we're trained to immediately think about 'what next?'. Within moments of his short resignation statement little huddles formed as discussion turned to who would replace him. It provided a welcome distraction from the expenses row and within a couple of hours three potential candidates had already sounded me out. By far the most preposterous suggestion was the offer from Ann Widdecombe to stand as interim Speaker, no doubt to be sponsored by a reality TV show.

When John Bercow called asking if I would back him my only hesitation was due to a promise I'd made to Ming Campbell. Having foolishly not backed him when he ran as leader of my party I wasn't going to make the same mistake again. In the end he decided not to run and I was able to offer full support to John. On the day itself the Speaker election boiled down to a choice described by my friend and colleague Paul Keetch as between 'the Baronet and the Boy'. Sir George Young made the best speech at the hustings and was both literally and metaphorically head and shoulders above the rest, but my judgement was that he was too safe a pair of hands. If we are to convince the outside world we are modernising, is a knight from Hampshire and Eton the best image? When he asked me to sign his nomination form it was with regret that I tried to point this out. He would bluntly have been a better choice for Speaker then Michael Martin ten years ago, but as often happens in life the combination of talent and timing had not worked in his favour. Bercow is a risk. Intelligent, he's a maverick who's passionate about Parliament but at forty-six represents a generation that wants to look beyond the wigs and tights.

Getting out of the silly clothes is important; a few years before Parliament looked bloody stupid when men in tights and swords attempted to arrest protesters as they stormed the Palace of Westminster. It all adds to the sense that we are out of touch – even the title 'Serjeant at Arms' sounds like something from a Gilbert and Sullivan opera. Incidentally, why could I never turn my radiator on or off without a direct order from the said Serjeant? For thirteen years I have either frozen or boiled in my office and had to purchase heaters or coolers.

The public anger over the expenses scandal made life tougher than normal away from the Westminster bubble. In my various charity board meetings the 'E-word' was nearly always the subject of great amusement. On the whole I was on the receiving end of light-hearted banter. My

Sunday league football team mates wasted no time in taking the mickey and I soon learnt it was best to get in first and try to make light of it all. At every Hampshire supper party I went to our friends all had an opinion. The surgeons, lawyers and bankers in our social set all sympathised at the awful level of pay I was on. I guess it's all relative but I am not sure the reaction would have been the same if I lived in a less affluent area. But imagine what it's like to go to supper or drinks when everybody has a view on your salary and expenses. You become the subject of discussion, which in my case I find terribly difficult. I am very shy and at private social events hate having the focus on me. I can appear in front of millions on TV or at a local public meeting but find eight people at supper difficult and I prefer to listen than be the centre of attention.

So for those that don't know what my job is I tend to dodge the subject. That's not always easy. At the height of the *Telegraph* stories Belinda and I took the children and some of their friends for a night's camping in the New Forest. Now, I hate camping at the best of times but this particular late May was boiling hot. I was already grumpy as I'd had my own *Telegraph* call that morning so was edgy about what they would print. The campsite was organic, which meant a hole in the ground and lots of sawdust. The meadow setting triggered a hay fever attack and one of Alice's friends started throwing up due to sunstroke.

At dusk Belinda decided to go all 'Kum Ba Yah' on me and got her guitar out to play in front of a camp fire. The music, or more likely the fire, drew a couple of fellow campers to join us. All of a sudden everything got a bit *Hi-de-bloody-Hi!* and I had to start being sociable. Half an hour in we established that she was a hairdresser and he ran a museum. Then the inevitable question for me: 'So what do you do then?' Silence. All you could hear was the fire crackling away. Belinda and Alice both glared at me and I jumped up announcing I was going to roast a marshmallow. That's how bad it's got – I couldn't face admitting I was a member of Parliament. Alice neatly summed it up the next day: 'Dad, I wouldn't have minded if you lied.' It was a truly awful time to be in the spotlight.

So how did Westminster get into this whole expenses mess in the first place? Well in my view, behind the whole scandal lay a fundamental problem of MPs' pay. If we are to attract good people into politics then the salary must increase. It may be a great starting level for a former researcher or policy worker but do we want to encourage more people like that into Parliament? When I was elected to Parliament I had to take a pay cut. It was ironic that I was paid more to try and influence politicians as a public affairs consultant than when I actually became a member. In the decade that followed my salary edged up bit by bit – some years MPs were too scared to vote themselves a raise, then in others we played catch-up. But compared to my peer group my salary was stuck. They were all getting promotion and seeing their income increase. For a man in his thirties, bringing up a family, the £60,000 salary of an MP was low compared to what all our friends were earning. I totally accept that this sounds greedy when compared to nurses or police officers but we need to treat MPs in line with similar positions in society, such as head teachers, doctors and business directors. It beggars belief that most local authority chief executives earn more than our Prime Minister – let alone an MP. We need to attract different people into Parliament; our country should be governed by individuals who've done something else in their lives. We need the forty- or fifty-year-olds to switch careers and move from running businesses, schools, the Army and hospitals to running the country. They will never do it on the current salary. They are also very unlikely to risk giving up a job and standing for Parliament, thinking of the long years campaigning in the constituency ahead of an election. They may even not fancy signing up to a political party. We are effectively ruling out the most highly skilled on the grounds of salary, party affiliation and a constituency-based system of elections.

The former CBI leader Digby Jones is a perfect example of this dilemma. I know and like Digby and there is no doubt of his value to Westminster. When we spoke during his time as leader of the CBI, he left me in little doubt that he didn't fancy finding a safe seat and getting involved in the cut and thrust of elections. His elevation to the Lords allowed him into government, but the system could not really cope with the concept that he would not sign up to join the Labour Party.

I am beginning to think the Lords has the potential to deliver a vehicle for bringing high-quality people into government. If we can encourage the middle-aged generation to suspend careers in return for a seat in the Lords that may be a price worth paying.

With its non-confrontational approach and bank of experience, much of what comes out of the Lords is a better model of government that some of the nonsense we produce at the other end of the building. However, the lack of democratic accountability is a rather obvious drawback. My preference would be to reform the Commons and radically reduce the number of MPs. We should move towards a structure that creates about 400 members. The constituency they represent would be larger, but they would be provided with fully staffed offices owned by government which are in place whoever the MP is.

Despite all these failings I've seen first hand that the vast majority of MPs are honest and hardworking. One of the motivations behind bringing out this book was to try and give an honest account of what it is really like to be a Member of Parliament. I collect political biographies but nearly all of them are the work of former Prime Ministers or senior public figures often keen to rewrite history and portray in a self-important way their version of historic events. I don't fall into that category and I certainly have not played any part in major historic events. So warts and all I've attempted to explain what being an MP is like. I am trying as best I can to let you into our world.

I guess the most demanding part is the diary. Each day you receive about ten requests to attend meetings, receptions, launches, conferences, visits, briefings, openings and seminars. I estimated in one year alone I was invited to more than 2,500 events. In the end you have to decide what to do. I throw a third in the bin, say no to another third and then try and fit the rest into my programme. Top priority is given to invitations in Winchester. Visiting the hospital or one of the 65 schools is important to keep in touch with public services. You try to build up good relations with the people in charge and I hope to gain their trust. When a couple of years ago two mothers died over the Christmas period after having babies at my local hospital I was able to offer supportive, not knee-jerk, responses as a result of the long-term relationship I have with the staff of the Royal Hampshire Hospital. When the parents of little Timothy are complaining about his education it helps if I can speak on first-name terms to the head of the school. As Winchester is home to the head offices of IBM, Arqiva, and Denplan amongst others it's also key that the MP visits and acts as a champion for business in his area.

Acting as a voice for local good causes is another part of the job. There are hundreds of voluntary groups in Winchester and I've attempted to visit many of them over the years. Often they want money and help with appeals in return. This means fund raising and that means being prepared to act daft. I've been dressed as a penguin, walked with a Teletubby and been thrown into jail all in the name of good causes! Representing a large rural constituency also means village fetes. This brings various hazards, the worst of which, for me, are the bloody Morris dancers. When I was elected, one of my first events was to open the fete in Wickham. Tradition has it that the member of Parliament leads the parishioners in the first Morris dance immediately after the opening. I performed this with reasonably good humour. A week later at a village nearby the same thing happened. I reported all this back to Belinda, who found it all rather amusing. Anyway the following weekend we'd been invited to open the regatta at Winchester College – surely a civilised event, until to my horror I saw the bloody Morris dancers in the distance. This time I went up to Mr Morris and said: 'Please, I've been a great sport the last two weeks. Will you announce that it's traditional for the MP's wife to lead off the first dance?' Bingo – that wiped the smile off her face. Actually, if truth be told, with time I became rather fond of smashing sticks and waving my handkerchief around in the air.

The fetes take up the summer weekends with a never-ending demand to make a funny speech as you open the event. Often I would take the children along, sometimes opening three fetes a day. On one occasion, just as I was saying that this particular fete was the best I'd been to, Alice unfortunately piped up: 'You said that at the last one, Daddy!' Thanks, Alice, no coconuts for you today! And as if that isn't enough, you have to endure a constant stream of Friday and Saturday nights delivering after-dinner speeches at local constituency fund raisers.

The correspondence MPs receive can be overwhelming. The combination of letters and emails comes to about 100 a day. Most are standard letter or postcard mailings asking you to ban hunting, support an asthma campaign, oppose a war, support the Gurkhas or introduce euthanasia. Then there is a wave of more complex stuff based on whatever portfolio you may hold in Westminster. When I spoke on disability the various charities would bombard me with briefings on upcoming legislation or campaigns on issues they wanted me to support. On top of all that there is the internal party stuff, as the Lib Dem campaign teams ask you to support a campaign for post offices, or the Whips' Office wants to know if you can make a key vote, or the local party in Winchester wants to arrange a canvass and leaflet drop. And as if this wasn't bad enough you then have, in my case, thirty Lib Dem Councillors all emailing with issues to do with their own wards.

Finally, the most important stuff – real problems from constituents. These come via email, post, phone and often in person in the middle of Tesco. People need help about everything you could ever dream of. Benefits, medical treatment, care of the elderly, special-needs children, housing, planning permission, pensions, child support payments, divorce, immigration application, finding a job and, sadly on the increase, serious financial and debt problems. It's an enormous workload and I depend on a superb team headed up by my secretary, Julia Harkness, along with Lyn Anderson, Joan Read, Pam Johns, Anna Drabble and a team of volunteers. Prior to this Gill Kilmartin ran my office for ten years. At Westminster I've been lucky enough to have had a long stream of wonderful researchers over the years. Many of them have become firm friends, like Owen Braben and Olly Kendall, who had to deal with my nightmare press stories and the pressure of covering the home affairs portfolio. Antonis Papasolomontos, my current researcher, is a calming influence on the office as he constantly reminds me to vote and ask questions and keeps my mind from thinking about life after politics. I can never thank them all enough.

Before long you can end up dashing around without setting your own agenda. I soon saw this problem after I was elected so one of the things I quickly decided to do was to spend a day a month in somebody else's job.

Screwing Up

It was great fun and you learnt more doing the job at the coal face than via a briefing from the managers.

A day with the dustmen (or waste managers as I believe we're meant to call them) was an experience. Constituents were bemused to see me collecting their bins, I was bemused at the soft porn pinned up in the cab of the dustcart and the bin men were amused at my efforts to jump in and out of the cab at six in the morning. By eleven the vehicle had broken down so thankfully the day was cut short.

I hate early starts so the prospect of another one, this time doing a round with the postman (or mail direction co-coordinators), didn't fill me with much joy. There was plenty of banter as I tried to decipher addresses and place the mail into the correct pre-delivery slots. The round itself was a disaster and to this day I owe the residents of Winnall Manor Road an apology for the letters I muddled up.

The checkout at Sainsbury's was stressful. I can't add up or use machines so trying to scan and punch in numbers as items of frozen peas and shampoo shot by felt rather like a cruel version of that final conveyor belt section of *The Generation Game*. I tell you what, though: if you want the local gossip the checkout girls at Sainsbury's know everything that's worth knowing.

Working behind the bar at the local pub was a bit similar, although this time I had to juggle money, glasses and strange combinations of drink. My several stints behind various bars have all been a great laugh and allowed constituents to take the mickey. It's an easy way to chat to people and I think helps break down some barriers and perceptions about stuffy MPs. I remember Lembit Öpik and me doing an evening the shift at my local student union bar. By eleven we were confident enough to try out a few Tom Cruise *Cocktail*-style stunts. Maybe the students wondered what these two sad old geezers were doing – but I learnt more about student views and worries behind the bar than I would have behind a desk. 'Days in the life' became a regular event and throughout the years I've spent time as a farmer, vet, teacher, bus driver, policeman and ambulance driver.

However busy I may be with my duties at Westminster I am constantly reminded that I am also playing a key role in many real-life dramas amongst my constituents. If you have read the Alan Clark diaries you will recall he showed a fair amount of contempt for his constituents, portraying them as an inconvenience that had to be endured in return for a seat at Westminster as every four years or so he was rudely interrupted by the irritation of needing their votes at election time. It's certainly true that around the bars of Westminster we share the horror stories of mad and demanding constituents, although most of the frustration is vented over local party activity and the tales of how local councillors are screwing up our re-election chances.

In Winchester I've been lucky to have a wonderful bunch of local party members and thankfully, despite my spectacular efforts to screw things up, my constituents have been a never-ending source of encouragement. Rather than getting me down they have provided the rock for my political life. It's not always been that way, though.

When I led a small group of councillors in Watford I spent most of my time just trying to hold the group together, even though there were only four of us. At least two threatened to quit or switch party. There would be screaming fits, calls at midnight lasting for hours and endless crisis. The only real comfort was knowing that the other political leaders had just the same problems with their own awkward squad. The endless meetings and one-to-one chats needed to calm things down can be exhausting and a real distraction.

Alongside all of this the MP is expected to act as a national party figure, attending Lib Dem conferences and events up and down the country, not to mention the demands of early morning radio and late night TV with news channels in between. Then on top of this as home affairs spokesman I'd fit in meetings with the Police Federation, the Association of Chief Police Officers, the prison unions, various drug charities, visits to police forces across the UK and victim support groups. Finally there was the Westminster legislative programme, endless bill committees, home affairs questions, all-party groups and my own party meetings to keep me busy. It's an enormous workload and bluntly it pisses me off when people criticise us as over-paid layabouts – most of them would not last a week!

During the expenses scandal period, a number of celebrity figures offered to stand for Parliament and one, Esther Rantzen, has indeed put herself forward. I don't think they would last a moment, getting bored after a couple of months of holding surgeries and drowning in a sea of correspondence.

It's a frantic lifestyle but there is also a lot of wasted time, as I am sure that much of what we do could be done by local councillors and there is a danger that we become merely a very well-paid wing of the local Citizens Advice Bureau. Whilst this keeps us in touch and means each day MPs understand how legislation set at Westminster, say on the Child Support Agency, impacts on constituents' real lives, we do need to think about how to manage our time better. One big difference would be to cut back on the utter rubbish spoken by so many MPs. A good third of what goes on in Parliament is a total waste of time. Each day thousands of words are spoken, questions tabled and meetings held, but if there was ever an audit to see what was gained in these hours it would find little evidence of value for money. The moment an MP utters words they are forgotten. I often wonder if the sole purpose of the chamber for some MPs is to indulge in their favourite pastime: listening to their own voice. The problem is simple. You're only really in the chamber if you're waiting to speak, so by definition you want the other speaker to hurry up, allowing more time for your own pearls of wisdom.

There are exceptions to this. In early 2008, I joined the Business and Enterprise Select Committee and I've seen at first hand just how hard select committee members work as part of an investigation. The process of calling witnesses to give evidence with the cross-examination that follows reveals all sorts of material. Members set aside political differences and the resulting reports are, in my judgement, one of the best things to come from the corridors around Parliament. The pity is that most of the well-argued recommendations remain just that – recommendations. Working cross-party also takes place in all-party groups, on subjects as diverse as beer, bridge and Botswana. These days there are far too many groups – but some can have a real impact.

One of the benefits of this job is the chance to take an issue and, via debates in Parliament, bring it to the attention of the minister and the media. Over the years I've ended up taking on a number of cases, from prisoners of war to free range chickens, hearing aids for war veterans to suicides in prison and the UK wine industry. It means you become a temporary expert on a wide range of subjects, never understanding a great deal of detail but enough to become rather a jack of all trades. Perhaps this is why MPs seem to have a view on everything – in a parliamentary career we will indeed have been asked to speak up on almost anything!

The problem is that one week you will be engrossed in the arguments surrounding a complex health funding formula, the next you're dealing with government policy on developing brownfield land. After ten years of this intellectual flitting from issue to issue the brain becomes full and the only way to survive is to delete knowledge. In other words I am great at grasping something fast and articulating it simply but then forgetting it quickly. It's a survival mechanism but it can be very frustrating when years later you try to recall details.

We could make changes that would improve the day-to-day workings of an MP. Changing the ridiculous 10 p.m. votes on Monday and Tuesday would be a start – but we need to go further. Genuine reform of Parliament is long overdue and by genuine I don't mean changing some obscure constitutional law that no-one has heard of after months of deliberations. This doesn't need to be a drawn-out process with endless reviews that get ignored. Instead there are some real practical changes that can be made straightaway.

We need to change the way in which we do business. The very look and sound of Parliament is straight out of *Jurassic Park*. For example, protocol forbids clapping on the floor of the Commons. In most areas of western life if you wish to approve of a speech or event applause is in order, but at Westminster it is ruled out of order, and instead we have to shout 'hear, hear'. It makes us sound like a bunch of farmyard animals and whilst it may be a crowd pleaser for tourists it does little to help our image.

I can recall a few exceptions, most notably when Robin Cook resigned from the government over the war in Iraq. His eloquent and well-argued speech, combined with the obvious personal political sacrifice he was making, resulted in a small ripple of applause which then grew into a standing ovation. It is to this day the only event in the Chamber which has moved me close to tears. There was also long applause for John Bercow when he was elected Speaker, perhaps signalling a break with the past.

It takes a few months to become familiar with all these little traditions. I'd assumed that each MP would have an allocated seat and was surprised to discover that to get a seat you need to obtain a prayer card in the morning and then turn up to pray as the House starts. If I thought that praying to reserve a seat was odd, the actual ceremony of the prayers themselves is an even stranger ritual, which involves turning around several times, bowing and praying to nearly everybody for what seems like an eternity.

It's time to move MPs into a modern parliament fit for the twenty-first century. The stiff green benches set opposite each other create a hostile atmosphere. They play to a two-party system and there are not enough places for everyone, which results in MPs sitting on the floor during the popular debates. It's ridiculous to have MPs pushing and shoving, virtually sitting on each other's laps with no place for laptops or briefing material all over your knees if you're lucky. The chamber is small – much smaller than I ever imagined it from the TV. When I first walked in as an MP, I was confused, thinking it was some kind of ante-room. Set on the floor as you enter is a big white line. You are meant to step and bow to the Speaker on entering and leaving at this point.

The way we vote, however, is the piece of nonsense that bugs me most. As a debate draws to a conclusion, the Speaker stands up and shouts: 'As many as those saying Aye, say Aye!' We all shout 'Aye', and then the same thing happens for a Noe. If there is shouting for both Aye and Noe then the Speaker bellows 'Division!' and the vote is on, bells ringing all over Westminster. We then have eight minutes to get from our office, committee room or TV studio to the entrance of the Commons. At this point each of the parties has a whip to direct its MPs down one of two corridors – Aye and Noe. As we push and shove our way down the corridor our aim is to get to the other end, where three clerks sit at desks and tick our names off a long list. But there remains one more hurdle. You then pass one by one through a door at which two MPs count you and in return you nod at them. This nodding dates back to an age when lazy MPs would send a butler to vote, so a nod was required to show your face and real identity. It's madness! It takes twenty minutes and, late at night especially, makes me feel grumpy when I know the whole thing could be done electronically within seconds.

As the public look down behind big glass screens they see a bunch of mainly men calling each other Honourable this, Right Honourable that, My Learned Friend, the Member for Winchester, Hull or Mid-Bedfordshire. The whole language sends totally the wrong message. We come across as out of touch, from a different world, more fit to be stuffed and put in a museum. With clerks in wigs and officials in tights running around it looks more like a sketch from *Blackadder*. The whole thing is enormously frustrating – as is the inability to change things.

If I look back over the situation in Winchester in the thirteen years since my election, to be honest things have become worse, not better. You can't travel from A to B without being caught in a traffic jam. The trains are late, full and expensive. We have ruined our green fields with new estates. We leave patients waiting for ages before ambulances turn up. Our school results get better but our school leavers can't seem to work in offices. Our drinking levels are out of control with fighting on the streets. I had a pensioner come into my surgery who couldn't find the money to get her oven fixed. She was able to claim special funds – but why the hell should she need to fill in a 31-page form? You can't register with an NHS dentist in most of my constituency. If your relatives need care at home you can't get help for them. If you want to send your children to the local school you may have a battle on your hands.

Nationally, we pay our farmers not to grow but to import food. We stop foreign nationals coming to their relatives' funerals yet we can't stop gang masters importing slave labour to pick cockles in Morecambe Bay. Our prisons are full and the most crowded in Europe – yet our reoffending levels are around 65 per cent. We're burdened with more and more rules and regulations from hunting and smoking to miles and miles of red tape that kill off small businesses.

Screwing Up

We spent the last decade pushing sport and fun out of education and are surprised that there is a generation growing up fat and depressed. Our students build up debts from fees which will stay with them for years. The biggest queue at the Winchester student freshers' fair used to be for free condoms and beer – now it's at the Manpower stand.

Our junior doctors end up paying for courses themselves to get essential training. The level of bugs and infections on our wards is at an all-time high. Divorced parents end up at war over bungled Child Support Agency claims. Thousands of people are asked to pay back tax credit overpayments and the state leaves private information about millions of benefit claimants lying around on trains. Councils have to wait for a serious accident before they find a scheme to improve road safety. And the very people whose job it is to fix all this are now regarded as second-class citizens, leaving our political institutions mistrusted with low voter turnouts.

Perhaps I am becoming a grumpy old man. As an MP for over a decade I have been able to see a lot of remarkable changes take place but when I leave office and step out of the Commons for the last time I will be walking away from a building and a process that has barely shifted. It's said that the British public like their pomp and pageantry but on the whole I think Parliament is out of touch, politicians are increasingly distrusted and the gulf between 'us' and the public is as broad as it has ever been. I wish I'd used the time to fight for more reform but like so many I think I just gave up.

However, looking to the future, the political landscape does seem set for change. The current government is running out of steam and it feels very like the dying days of the John Major government in the mid-1990s. The economic downturn and the expenses scandal have created an atmosphere of gloom with every opinion poll showing that Gordon Brown's days are numbered. Meanwhile the arrival of David Cameron onto the political scene has given the Conservatives new life and the prospect of power. My own party remains resilient and as the pendulum of politics begins one of its regular swings between the main parties, the Liberals look set to remain a large third force. However, the shift between the two big parties brings with it some tough challenges for Nick Clegg. The last four or five elections have seen the growth of tactical voting as the voters opposed to the 'nasty' Tory Party learnt to pick which of the Labour and Liberal Democrat candidates stood the better chance of ousting a Conservative. This resulted in an increase in the Liberal Democrat vote in a significant number of Tory seats and helped grow the number of MPs steadily over the last five elections. Now the Tories are the 'nice' party, this tactical vote looks set to disappear and make for some tough Liberal–Tory scuffles in marginal seats. That said, I know that my fellow Liberal Democrat MPs work extremely hard for their constituents and what's become known as the incumbency factor should see most of them hold on.

In fact it's far from all bad news for Clegg and Co. next time round. Whilst voters may leak to the Tories I don't see it turning into a flood – they are still not trusted by many, and Labour's increasing unpopularity could see the Lib Dems picking up seats to compensate for any losses to the Tories.

Nick is of course aware that he is performing a high-wire act but he is well placed to deal with the twin challenge of communication and intellectual ability. He looks and sounds normal and whilst he is not a nerdy swot, his brain is more than capable of developing a set of positions for the party that move them on from the rather crude tax-and-spend approach that many of our spokesmen have argued for. His handling of the Gurkhas' claim for citizenship and calls for the Speaker to resign in the spring of 2009 and his courage to question the level of support for troops in Afghanistan showed an ability to be in touch with the public mood and speak for reform. I am a big fan of his and believe the public will warm to him when they see him on a daily basis during the election campaign.

If the Tories fail to storm home, then Clegg's biggest challenge by far will be the prospect of a hung parliament. Ending up as kingmaker brings with it a set of opportunities only matched in magnitude by the enormous dangers the third party would face. At best it could deliver credibility, power, policy gains and PR; at worst it could result in a split party, leading to electoral ruin. No wonder then that Kennedy, Campbell and Clegg have all tended to avoid detailed public discussion about the prospects of a close election. Even to acknowledge the possibility is seen as admitting defeat and draws the party into discussions over deals in what would have been smoke-filled rooms at a time when party leaders want to focus on their own agenda without being hijacked.

A hung Parliament was not a realistic outcome under the Kennedy leadership so he was able to declare there would be no deals without much challenge. The problem for Clegg is that the next election could be close. He just can't get away with a position that claims no interest in forming a coalition or pact. It would be highly irresponsible if the electorate voted for a draw to allow the county to drift from one parliamentary vote to another without at least explaining the option of creating some parliamentary arrangement to provide stability and an agreed Queen's Speech.

I find it inconceivable that Clegg would decide to keep Gordon Brown in power if he lost his overall majority at the next election. The electorate will have delivered their verdict and any attempt by the Lib Dems to defy that and give Labour a fourth term would be severely punished at a future election – obtaining proportional representation in return would be no compensation for the fall-out. I don't even think he could take the whole party with him. A small group of more economic-minded Liberals may very well be tempted to pull away and work for the Tories. It's not only the electoral disadvantages that direct my thinking. I just don't think four-term governments of any political persuasion are good for the country. Three-term governments are bad enough – look at Thatcher and Blair. But the worst recent precedent for a government going well beyond its sell-by date is the Major government, which managed to hang onto power against all the odds for a painful five years after surprising everybody by winning in 1992.

I don't want Brown clinging to power in this way with the help of Lib Dem MPs. If I was staying in the next Parliament I would argue strongly that the party should look to oust Labour and if the arithmetic works come to an arrangement with the Conservatives. There will be a powerful case for a fresh start and the Lib Dems should embrace rather than resist that.

It may have been unthinkable pre-Cameron to consider a deal with the Conservatives but things have changed. As Liberals we share some common territories. During my time as home affairs spokesman I found that the true partners in defending liberal values were the Conservatives. Against all my expectations, I get on well with David Davis, labelled in the press as 'a right-wing pro-hanger'. I found him impressive and liberal. When we were involved in some of the detailed discussions following the London terrorist attacks, he held firm on issues such as holding terror suspects for ninety days. In fact, on more than one occasion, I was the one wobbling and prepared to compromise. When he resigned his seat to make a stand over the government's increasing authoritarianism, I had no hesitation in travelling north to help campaign for him in his by-election. Driving round in a blue battle bus was slightly odd but it was for a good cause. He would have made a good Home Secretary.

Although the Tories initially supported both ID cards and the war in Iraq, they are now against both and their position has moved closer to the Liberal Democrats'. On the environment they are moving in the right direction with a clear commitment and even on Europe the Liberals have strong allies in the Ken Clarke wing of the party. They are not and never will be an alternative to a genuine radical Liberal Party but it would be churlish not to acknowledge that they are a different party these days and we should not dismissing the option of working with them.

I will not be standing at the next election – the first time in over two decades that I won't be an elected politician. It's an extraordinary experience to seek and then get the support of your fellow citizens and I've been lucky enough to win six out of the seven elections I've fought. It will be strange not to feel nervous at the count, peculiar not to go through the exhaustion and emotions of the campaign trail. My Winchester seat disappears at the next election, turning into two new constituencies. I hope the Liberal Democrat candidates picked to replace me go on to win the seats. I hope Nick Clegg has a good election and the Liberals grow in influence at Westminster. For the sake of the country though, I hope we have a clear result, an end to Labour and a fresh start with a government of authority and a Parliament reformed, fresh and ready to restore credibility to our democratic process.

11

Happy again – I think

Time has moved on and in nearly every aspect of life I am happier now than in those years when I was in front-line politics. That's not to say that everything is forgotten, forgiven or resolved in my life; far from it. Things come back to haunt me – simple daily tasks like opening the bedroom curtains on a Saturday are a reminder of the morning when I woke to find reporters outside my house. Each week the press cuttings still contain some reference to my scandal and in the goldfish bowl that is Westminster there are daily reminders of the past life in the fast lane. Writing this book will drag things up again, but I hope in doing so I can end a chapter and signal that I've moved on.

When I have a bad day Belinda reminds me how it was in the months after I was exposed. In that bitterly cold spring, I hated going out, I was hardly eating, taking sleeping tablets, sleeping alone and facing an uncertain future.

Rebuilding a relationship, career and self-esteem needs the support of friends, family, professionals and colleagues. I am grateful to have had all of that. For Belinda's family it's been very tough. Hampshire farmers are more at home dealing with real rats than love rats. I don't think things will ever be the same again with them. They will rightly never quite trust me and I will always feel I let them down. That said, Belinda's mother has been truly remarkable. She's Dutch and despite her rural lifestyle maintains a continental liberal attitude which has grown the older she gets. Far from becoming more intolerant, she's been able to deal with the bizarre goings-on of her youngest son-in-law with a generosity, kindness and warmth I will never forget. Such is her forgiveness that she was even able to hug me within moments of being told the news. My own mother has also shown unquestionable support and always stood by me at the worst times, giving unconditional love.

Political colleagues have also been generous. When I resigned my postbag was full of private notes sent by all kinds of MPs, from Cabinet ministers to opposition frontbenchers. In particular Conservative backbenchers wrote in large numbers and very movingly, some telling of their own problems and offering names of people who might help. I'd never been a great note writer when a fellow MP was in trouble, but when I was up against it these letters meant a great deal. There was an interesting common theme – 'There but for the grace of God go I'. I now always try to drop a note to a colleague or public figure in deep water. I might not approve of what they've done but I'd have to be very hard not to feel sympathy.

I am not the first or last political figure to fall from grace and perhaps that should have been a warning to me. But I had never felt in the same league as some of the big political beasts caught with their pants down. I can remember as a nineteen-year-old student at Wall Hall College going to listen to the local MP, Cecil Parkinson, give a talk just a week after he resigned as Tory Party chairman following a sex scandal. Even then I felt sympathy for him as he stood in front of a bunch of students looking and sounding every bit a broken man. I can remember during John Major's final years feeling no great joy at the problems faced by David Mellor and Tim Yeo as they admitted high-profile affairs. These should have all acted as warnings to me but sadly the brain doesn't work that way. In fact I think there is something about the political world that almost draws politicians into relationship problems. Not long after my affair broke I was interviewing the ex-Tory MP Michael Brown, himself the subject of a *News of the World* exposé, as part of a film I was making for *Newsnight*. He said that risk taking made him a good politician but of course those same risks worked less well in his private life. The modern political animal is a risk taker; you have to be to stand for public office in the first place and deal with a level of public interest. I think this in part explains why so many MPs throughout the world end up in trouble with colourful private lives. There are the obvious candidates: outgoing types such as Alan Clark, Boris Johnson or my mate Lembit Öpik. However, who would have thought of John Major, John Prescott or dull old Mark Oaten? Perhaps it's just in the DNA of all politicians.

Over the years people tend to remember you did something wrong but can't quite pin down what it was. As you fade from memory a new victim comes along and becomes the talk of Westminster. Not long after I was exposed, the Tory MP Greg Barker was found to have a secret male lover and then John Prescott's affair with his secretary was disclosed. On both occasions the press made contact with me to get my view on the latest affairs. It's as if you've become an expert on scandal – in the space of a few months I'd gone from Lib Dem home affairs spokesman to, well, just affairs spokesman.

Part of me would like to know how others survive – to share tips or attend a masterclass on scandal. I've spoken with a few other victims about this and exchanged emails with Max Mosley on the subject. As I look ahead I am aware that the track record of those other fallen figures is patchy to say the least. David Mellor moved into broadcasting, combining his passions for football and music. Cecil Parkinson went to the House of Lords and has not really been heard of since. Others, such as Neil Hamilton, have become celebrity fodder, moving from quiz to panto with a brave face. Many people warned me not to 'do a Hamilton', muttering that it was disgusting. I disagree. I am full of admiration for Neil and Christine. They brushed themselves down and got out there to make a living. Why should they just hide away? They needed the money and I suspect it gave them something positive to focus on. For Jonathan Aitken, the focus was on jail and religion. His autobiography mainly chronicles the events that took him from rising to fallen star, but it was sent to me by a number of people urging me to turn to Christ as Aitken did. I am pleased to see the Conservatives have asked him to advise them on penal reform.

Jeremy Thorpe never recovered from his court case and scandal, which rocked the Liberals in the mid-1970s. The flamboyant and colourful leader was defeated at the 1979 election after his exposure and has never been elevated to the Lords by subsequent party leaders. I went to see him in the spring of 2007 to interview him for my book on coalitions. I wanted to find out what really happened when he and Ted Heath spoke about a possible coalition after the first knife-edge election of 1974. I found Thorpe sitting at his desk in his study surrounded by portraits, photos and memorabilia of a career which was cut short in one of the most famous scandals of all time. Suffering from Parkinson's, he could hardly talk and was terribly weak. It was a tragedy. He muttered that he doubted if the party would wish him to help at the next election. I left his mews house near Hyde Park upset that over thirty years later he looked so haunted by the past.

Similarly, the past never left the man involved in the most famous downfall of them all. In the list of all scandals nothing has topped John Profumo; even after his death his very name remains a byword for disgrace. Despite his years of quiet public service and charitable work he was never allowed to escape his affair with Christine Keeler. The bitchy diarists kept telling me to disappear and do the decent thing like Profumo. Why, for what purpose? The press never let him forget. I've a family to raise, I want to keep working – and as I keep having to remind myself, yes, I screwed up but I've not committed murder.

So the track record to recovering is not easy. Life after scandal is tough.

Part of the recovery is to understand that you've made the mistake and not lash out and blame everybody else. As Jonathan Aitken said, 'The number one priority is genuine repentance … an acceptance that you and you alone have cocked your life up … Don't waste time blaming the deckhands and sub-lieutenants.' He's right. It would be far too easy to walk away sticking imaginary pins into a tabloid editor. The danger is that bitterness could last for life. I think a bout of self-pity is unavoidable and part of moving on, but to hold those feelings for too long is destructive. It really is a case of picking yourself up – but the body tells you something else. In the immediate weeks after the *News of the World* stories about me I wanted to crawl into bed and sleep. This is not uncommon. Christine Hamilton, quoted in the play *Life After Scandal* by Robin Soans, said: 'I didn't get out of bed for some days. I could only sleep with sedation. I didn't go to the supermarket. I didn't go out. I spent most of the time sitting in an armchair just staring ahead; just staring at the wall, motionless, staring at the floor.' For some this low point can result in suicidal thoughts. Jonathan Aitken said he definitely contemplated jumping off a cliff in northern California.

You also find suddenly that you have become public property. People you have never heard of have an opinion about you. A few weeks after I was in all the papers I went to the Sainsbury's near my London flat. The place nearly came to a standstill with people stopping to stare, point and grab friends and relatives to come and look at me. It was terrifying. I kept my head down, gathered a few basics and rushed out. I accepted that, but what I found hardest was not being able to speak to them all, answer back, explain or justify. In particular the nonsense on the internet hurt but it was pointless to try and respond.

To your face, journalists, fellow MPs and business contacts are wonderfully supportive – and to be fair in my case I have never experienced an old contact avoiding meeting my eye or not returning calls. There is, however, a sense that the 'Establishment' does become nervous. You're clearly damaged goods and although individually people are willing to forgive and focus on your qualities they are collectively nervous. Neil Hamilton summed it up when, also in *Life After Scandal*, he said: 'The Establishment is and always has been more interested in preserving the integrity of institutions than any notion of justice for the individual … put the stone across the vault … you have to be buried never to be revived.'

But is all of this in the public interest? Should public figures have to step down as a result of their sexual exploits? It's unusual for businessmen to get involved in scandals and I can see little justification for the press exposing the private lives of either Max Mosley or Lord Browne, the former BP boss. After all they are accountable to shareholders but not the public. What goes on between their bed sheets is less important than what appears on the balance sheets in my view.

What then of that other group who regularly find themselves in the Sunday exclusives – the pop and showbiz stars? Here I have less sympathy. Unlike those in the corporate world, these well-paid stars live for publicity and know the price of fame. They're unlikely to lose a job and in most cases will exploit the publicity gained from a fling to enhance their career. If the press want to discuss Katie and Peter's private lives, well, so be it; I think they signed away their right to privacy when they signed the rights to a fly-on-the-wall documentary.

That leaves the politicians. Hardly a month goes by when one of our elected representatives doesn't end up finding themselves caught out. But does it matter? I think there are a few basic tests.

The first is the Ken Livingstone point, when it was revealed he had slept with several women – as he rightly said, he broke no laws. This is important as politicians are also legislators and it would be hard to continue in high office if you were convicted of a serious crime. The second test is hypocrisy. This is not so black and white, but if an MP who went out of his way to campaign against drugs was caught taking them he should probably be exposed and fall on his sword. Linked to this is the question of lying and deceit. It's often been said that Profumo lying to Parliament was a bigger sin than his actual relationship with Keeler. The third and final test is judgement. If a politician opens himself up to blackmail as a result of an affair this can be regarded as bad judgement or in my case deciding to run for leadership of a political party when there was a skeleton hidden away. When I was exposed by the *News of the World* I felt strongly I should resign from front-line politics as it raised questions about my judgement – and to be honest I was so shattered I just wanted to give it all up.

But if you can pass these three tests then I can't see the need to resign over a private affair. At the end of the day what matters is the quality of the job performed by that individual. And here's the catch. It's often the colourful side to politicians that make them popular. We are endlessly told that the public want Westminster to reflect the real world. Well, you can't have MPs as real human beings without also accepting their odd private lives as well.

When I resigned the vast majority of the 8,000 emails and letters I received were supportive and this suggests to me that despite loving to read about private lives the voters are very forgiving and would much rather judge a politician on his or her record. So whilst I don't think we will stop the stories, let's at least stop the knee-jerk resignation calls.

I make no excuses for what I have done or the role the press has had in my scandal and withdrawal from frontbench political life. I don't think I am in a position to blame the press for my actions and in many ways, strange as it may seem, the whole episode has left me stronger and in a more stable state than before. But even so I think I am entitled to say that sometimes the press, particularly the tabloids and certain writers, have gone too far. And I would be lying if I said that the continued coverage, innuendos and suggestive commentary don't become draining from time to time. I am, however, in a position to look back and reflect on what this says about today's media.

After thinking about all the arguments surrounding privacy versus public interest, I've decided to come down against a privacy law. It would hinder the freedom of the press too much and I don't think I am comfortable with that idea. The media perform an important function in the democratic process, sometimes holding ministers and government to account more effectively and certainly more loudly than the elected opposition. The press help to investigate and expose a good number of scandals and issues which need to be confronted and brought out into the open. If the media have made a few mistakes, pushed boundaries beyond acceptable levels in a few high-profile cases in the past, then that, I suppose, is the price to be paid for the sleaze and corruption they have unearthed in others. It's not an easy conclusion to come to after my own experience but I think it's the right one. But the press must always remember that what they do to sell a paper for just one day can leave somebody else picking up the pieces for a whole lifetime.

In my case, about four months after I'd resigned things started to calm down at Westminster. There were key steps along the way that helped. Being asked back on to *Question Time* felt like an important step towards being accepted again. Another key turning point was the offer from BBC2's *Daily Politics* to take part in a six-week series on MPs getting fit. My office was dead against me doing anything other than hiding away, but I felt this would be a great chance to actually get fit and at least the publicity would be about my weight, not my sex life.

The programme involved four MPs being sent to a 'body doctor' who put us through our paces at Chelsea Football Club's training centre. The body doctor, David Marshall, turned out to be a natural television personality, but with a serious edge. He was determined to get across a message to politicians about children and fitness and if that meant killing a few Honourable Members in the process, so be it. His previous victims included Chelsea footballers and the television duo Ant and Dec. I went into the programme nervous and lacking any real confidence. Each day we pushed out press-ups and lifted weights beyond our wildest dreams, and I swore and moaned to such a degree that most of my gym work had to be edited out for daytime TV! By the end I felt better about myself and had lost almost a stone in weight.

David taught me that with a bit of self-discipline and commitment I could achieve anything. I started off able to do just five press ups. By the end of six weeks I could do sixty. The whole exercise routine became a real drug for me as it released natural energy into my body and stopped me drinking for the longest period since I'd become a member of Parliament.

After the programme finished I decided to keep at the gym. I found a personal trainer called Louis at my local gym in Winchester and my weekly Friday session has become a real life saver. I owe a great deal to the body doctor and now Louis for putting up with my constant complaints and keeping me healthy in mind and body.

Sport has become a way of learning to relax. As well as the gym session, I started tennis lessons with a guy called Alex whose aim is to help me beat the Hampshire housewives in their various charity events. He's a great teacher and even allows me to win the odd point. Both Louis and Alex could easily have refused to help this scandal-ridden MP. Instead without hesitation they've become part of the routine that has got me back on my feet.

More recently I've joined the House of Commons football team and for the first time in my political life find myself on the left wing. It's great fun and the cross-party approach means you're playing alongside ministers and political opponents. My office were slightly bemused to get an official ministerial response on a constituent problem with a handwritten note from the minister at the bottom apologising for missing a goal after my pass!

I've also had more time to enjoy the garden and greenhouse, recently adding chickens to the 'good life'. Actually, the hens can be a bit of a nightmare, particularly if they are broody. We had one who sat on her nest for a month, not moving an inch. This caused much controversy amongst the sudden plethora of chicken experts advocating very different policies on dealing with a broody individual. Panic was raised by a friend who said the hen would die if not lifted and encouraged to eat. My mother-in-law dismissed this as nonsense and advised me just to leave her alone (the chicken, not my mother-in-law!).

After a lot of debate and with considerable difficulty I lifted her off and attempted to get her exercising. Imagine if you'd been sitting still for a month – it was like watching someone get out of a car after a long journey. After a few lazy stretches she started running around and clearly enjoyed the freedom. It's been great fun and I wish we had more spare time to branch out beyond chickens.

Of course the biggest challenge has been to my relationship with Belinda. Within weeks of the scandal emerging I made contact with Relate. Belinda was insistent we should get help and had tried to get me to Relate a few years before, but now I had no hesitation in seeking support. We found a superb counsellor near Victoria and then, after she left, at the Tavistock Centre in Swiss Cottage. These weekly sessions were a wonderful way to deal with not just what happened, but much more.

I would frankly recommend a mid-marriage Relate session to anybody, irrespective of a crisis. The sessions are, of course, totally confidential and non-judgemental and they allowed us the space to explore what had gone right and wrong in each week as we started to rebuild our relationship. The fifty minutes spent facing our counsellor produced laughter and tears, but never in two years an argument, although we heard some furious rows coming from along the corridor as other couples become rather vocal. At times it can be frustrating. If you are looking for answers, or clear-cut rights and wrongs, they don't leap out and your counsellor is most certainly not a referee. I often asked what is normal to be told nothing is – it's what works for you! I think at times we would turn up wanting to be told off, or given clear instructions to do this or that, but you have to put more energy in yourself and figure it out. Some weeks it was emotionally draining and I found it hard to catch the Tube back to Westminster and go straight into meetings. Other times I would sit in the chair not really knowing what new to say. I often pleaded that we've talked about things hundreds of times, but then I have a tendency to gloss over things without getting into depth. It was a real security blanket and we were very nervous when the sessions finally ended towards the end of 2008.

Belinda has dealt with my failings over the whole period with remarkable strength. She is a unique girl. Born the youngest of five girls into a farming family she was a bit of a rebel from the start. Hardly out of nappies she was stealing her dad's cigars, teasing her sisters, and just generally letting the rest of the Fordham family know she had arrived. She even put an SDP poster up in 1981 in a defiant gesture against the sea of Tory blue that surrounded the farmhouse.

She was not going to play the Mrs Mellor game of publicly standing by her man with cups of coffee at the garden gate for the journalists. She was furious and hated the political world for the way in which it had encroached on our time. If she was going to stay with me it would be for her, us and our children, not some career-saving photo call.

Belinda and I are an odd match. We're opposites. She is outgoing, creative, disorganised and loves partying and spontaneity. I am shy, structured and just can't let go and have fun. If for example she persuades me to go to a festival or concert I dread having to dance in public. I'll hang around at the back of the tent or hall as Belinda seeks to surge forward and shows no inhibitions. It's either a great balance or a mismatch depending on the various ebbs and flows of our relationship. Marriage is a series of phases, waves, ups and downs, falling in and out of sync over the years, maybe even in and out of love, be it physical or emotional. But whatever the various points we've been at, friendship has remained at the heart. She is quite simply my best mate, and always will be.

My resignation from front-line politics gave us a chance to spend more time together. In 2006 we decided to take a long break during the party conference season, which had always clashed with our wedding anniversary. For nearly twenty-five years I've spent my Septembers at some God-awful seaside resort. Now the last thing I wanted to do was face the party faithful and the last thing the party wanted was to have me in town. It was the perfect time to have a two-week break. We'd always wanted to visit the Far East and now we had the time and money, thanks to Belinda's various interviews. We settled on a three-leg trip, starting with the big cities of Hong Kong and Bangkok and then a week on the beach in Phuket. We fell in love with the buzz of Hong Kong and I could never get enough of the wonderful skyline at night. Things were a bit more dramatic when we landed in Bangkok, where we found ourselves in the middle of what must have been the most polite and friendly military coup in history. Heading into the city from the airport Belinda delighted in pulling over the car and asking if she could climb on a tank and have her photo taken with the soldiers. I was my usual cautious self and hung back, expecting her to be marched off to the infamous 'Bangkok Hilton' for a six-month stay. Instead, true to form, she charmed the troops and within minutes was swinging a Kalashnikov from the top of the tank with the young army recruits more interested in trying to get in the photo than any fighting or uprising. The press back home hammed it all up – 'Oatens caught in military coup', 'Bad luck for couple as they try to patch up marriage', all that kind of stuff. In fact it was one of the happiest times of my life and the adventures of a coup, riding elephants and mopeds and lying on the beach were yet another important step in rebuilding our relationship.

The last few years have also given me a chance to become a better parent and enjoy watching Alice and Milly grow up. I missed too many school plays, parents' evenings and bath times during my time at Westminster. Although I've struggled with getting older myself, the one positive is being a good dad and watching my girls grow up themselves.

Whatever my failings as a husband I hope that I am a good parent. There's nothing I look forward to more than treating Alice to a shopping trip or allowing Milly to climb all over me. I dread the thought of them getting older and leaving home. I would freeze time, keeping them at thirteen and ten – old enough to engage, young enough to play.

Around Westminster I've found new interests. In particular, I was asked to join the Council of Europe, a rather unknown body in this country that pulls together all forty-eight geographical member states of Europe. Its great advantage is to get countries such as Russia and Georgia round the table. I attend various meetings on defence issues moving around European capitals and tend to be abroad almost every week. The UK delegation is led by John Prescott and I've become rather a fan. His blunt-speaking approach cuts through to the point and he chairs the meetings very well. In every sentence one or two words may be muddled up, but so what? It's clear he is a formidable political operator and our group in Europe is the better for his leadership. The Council of Europe also carries out election monitoring and early in 2009 I decided to put on the official jacket and head for Montenegro.

The country is a fusion of old-style communism and western shoe shops. The outskirts of the capital, Podgorica, are full of Soviet-style tower blocks but once you get to the centre you've never seen so many pairs of Converse and Adidas on sale in your life. I sometimes get terribly homesick in the first hours of landing in unknown places. This feeling is deepened if, as in Podgorica, the hotel and surrounding areas are depressing. The Crna Gora Hotel was horrid with a squeaky bed and no bath plug – although, to be fair, as there was no hot water for two days the plug was irrelevant. The TV could pick up three channels of the most hideous Europop or badly dubbed dramas.

A key part to election observation takes place in the run-up to polling day, which in this case was Sunday 29 March. On the Friday and the Saturday we had back-to-back meetings with the leaders of all thirteen political parties, the media and the various human rights pressure groups. A common theme emerged: 'You're too late – all the corruption and vote fixing took place weeks ago.' Bluntly they told us that everything would be fine on the day as the authorities would put on a good show for us. To help with the monitoring I was teamed up with Fidias, a member of Parliament from Cyprus, and in turn we were allocated our driver, Vladimir, and interpreter, Nicoloff.

The election was held the night before the Italian football team arrived to play a World Cup qualifier in the capital. Vladimir told me it was the biggest event for years and they were proud to host the match. He was anxious to get me a ticket and had contacts on the black market that could find one even though the match was sold out. I quickly pointed out that as an election observer my job was to fight corruption, not help feed the underworld! Instead I joined some locals who'd not been able to get a ticket and in a bar under the glare of the stadium floodlights we watched the match. We couldn't communicate much but I think they appreciated my occasional oohs and ahs as Montenegro put up a brave fight, outplaying the world champions but still losing 2-0.

It started to pour down as we headed out of the hotel with Vladimir and Nicoloff early on polling day. The car windows were steamed up, the road was bumpy and they were both smoking heavily. It was clearly going to be a testing day. Our first task was to oversee the official opening of a polling station which had been randomly selected for us. Turning up unannounced you could see the look of dread on the faces of the polling officials: why oh why us? In some polling stations, observers reported seeing voters taking photographs of their own ballot paper in the booth. They then went outside, passed the camera to a bunch of heavies waiting in a car and, having provided the evidence of voting for candidate X, collected their money.

We spent most of our day about one hour away from Podgorica in the northern region surrounding the city of Nikšić. Our tour around the polling stations took us through mountainous landscapes still tipped with snow in late March and full of rugged half-built houses with children and dogs running wild at the roadside. We found that in some of the polling stations the ballot boxes were not sealed. It wasn't difficult to spot; I just marched up and lifted the top of the box and saw all the votes inside. We asked polling staff to seal the boxes in front of us and with a combination of cigarette lighters, wax and string, boxes throughout the Nikšić region became secure under our watchful eye. The major obstacle to our work was Vladimir, who was insistent that we sampled the local food and beer at every step. After every polling station he directed us to the nearest cafe. The food was typical east European, heavy meat with slabs of cheese, creamy sauce and boiled potatoes, all washed down with Nik Gold, the local brew. I left the country feeling bloated and exhausted but at least I'd done my bit for democracy.

In recent years I have also had the chance to discover Africa and was lucky enough to visit Kenya as part of a Commonwealth parliamentary delegation at the end of 2008. Within hours of landing we were heading off into the countryside. Travelling high above the Nairobi we had the most wonderful view of the Rift Valley. Created from a massive split in the earth centuries ago, it runs from northern Syria to Mozambique. Our journey took us into the valley to a camp for displaced people who fled cities around Kenya during the post-election civil war of spring 2008. As so often happens on these occasions we arrived with a police escort and the refugees crowded round to provide a singing and cheering welcome. It never fails to both move me and make me feel awkward at the same time. There's a horrid imperial sense of superiority as the police chief informs them how grateful they should be that we've visited.

Wandering around the camp I came across an elegantly dressed man and asked him his story. He'd been a successful businessman running a number of cloth shops. When the violence broke out he was split from his wife and six children and for months each assumed the other had died. Happily he was united with his family when he ended up at the camp. Showing me round his UN-supplied tent all he had were a few blankets and pots. He'd lost everything else – except, thankfully, his family.

The next day we headed out to see some projects set up to help orphans. These were mainly run by religious groups and all set in very bleak and remote rural locations. After a dreadful journey, long and bumpy, we reached the end of the track and arrived at a small school. I was exhausted and felt close to passing out in the 40-degree heat as we were standing around. We looked at a few makeshift classrooms and then went on to a small room to meet a group of eight children who were infected with Aids. They were sat making beads and incredibly shy, with good reason, as we all crowded round to see them. They had exactly the same school uniform as Milly – but otherwise these youngsters led lives a million miles apart from my thankfully healthy, wealthy, cheerful daughter. They looked scared and haunted and it was a struggle to get a smile as they so clearly feared strangers.

Speaking to the family that ran the orphanage as we walked round, I was overwhelmed by their commitment to the children. At one point the mother drew me outside on the balcony of the doctor's surgery and it gave me an opportunity to ask them both just what it was like during the civil war. It was a story that left me lost for words.

Towards the end of the conflict rebel soldiers were getting closer and closer to the school and sporadic gunfire was becoming louder. In fear they took all the children into a room below the kitchen and told them to hide under the tables and keep very quiet. The rebels arrived at the school gate and the staff did their best to try and persuade them not to enter the grounds. Elsewhere these men had shown no mercy towards children and the staff must have been petrified at what atrocity they would commit if they found the hidden children. Thankfully the government forces arrived just in time and killed the rebels. For the Christian staff this was a dreadful choice but they remain grateful the rebels were killed.

It wasn't the only awful story I was told. A few days after the rebel attack a woman turned up at the school asking them for a safe haven. She arrived with nothing but a box which she said held all her belongings. She then opened it to reveal the head of her husband, who had been hacked to death days before.

Thankfully I provided the visit with a lighter moment. The children were showing us how they made soap and were busy stirring a bubbling green liquid as part of the process. I'd misunderstood, thinking it was soup, which explained the rather bemused looks when I asked if I could have a spoon to taste it!

Screwing Up

Kenya is a wonderful country but I was appalled at the levels of corruption we found and the failure of the politicians to learn from the uprisings after the election. The country now has a fragile coalition in place and when we met with the President and the Prime Minister they both said that they had looked over the edge of the precipice and would not go back. A year on, however, the situation remains volatile. The slightest event could trigger a civil war and the new wave of politicians elected to create a fresh start appear to be falling into bad ways.

I was to return to Africa a few months later when I was asked to visit Chad to see how the European Union Force joint military operation was working in this troubled region.

Flying in a military plane is, I imagine, not unlike the experience a suitcase goes through. We were strapped to the sides of the plane with an orange mesh similar to the tape used to cordon off roadworks. The initial shock of sitting staring inwards is compounded by a realisation that you're going to be sat on a wooden bench without a movie, drink or loo break for three hours. We made a few feeble jokes about the lack of trolley service before most of my fellow European parliamentarians ended up slouched, snoring and dribbling for most of the journey. The view from the windows was worth staying awake for. The endless nothingness was in its own way breathtaking as we flew over a red rocky and sandy terrain that looked like images of the surface on Mars. Occasionally a few goats would come into sight and as the shadow of our plane passed over the desert they would scatter, panicked at the sight of this animal with enormous wings. The goats would often be the first indication that a small settlement was nearby. These consist of a few round huts protected by a low brick wall marking out the village boundary, proving yet again that man's instinct from Chad to Chingford is to create a territory, whether from mud or leylandii. The figures around the camp seemed uninterested in the military planes overhead, I guess a reality of a war-torn region.

We descended into Abéché, which was little more than a strip of flattened sand. As we scrambled down the steps we were very quickly ushered into tanks and taken a short distance to the military camp. The tanks were driven by the Polish military who didn't break into a smile at any point during our stay and seemed to enjoy regularly pointing Kalashnikovs at us to make us shut up, put cameras away and get into the tanks quickly without banging our heads – a challenge for a couple of rather large Belgian parliamentarians, who'd clearly enjoyed sampling their national drink for too many years. Inside the tank the noise of the wheels on rough terrain was obliterated by a constant blast of Europop from the radio.

We were greeted in camp by the Irish commander, who took us immediately to our sleeping quarters. Now you need to remember that travelling MPs are more used to being checked into five-star hotels. Here our hotel turned out to be a massive tent with half a dozen camp beds and a kit bag. Immediately the cries went up: 'Where's the minibar?' 'There's no chocolate under the pillow! Hang on, there's no pillow!' The British MPs took it all quite well – our colleagues from across the Channel looked horrified at the prospect of a night under canvas.

I was enormously impressed with the way the European forces had pulled together. In total twelve countries were taking part. The Polish ran the tanks, the Croatians looked after surveillance, the Spanish flew the helicopters and thankfully the French did the cooking! Sadly, though, the region remains troubled and United Nations forces have now stepped in. Meeting them in New York a year later I was flabbergasted to learn that the French simply refused to hand over their equipment to the incoming UN force – instead they gave control of the airport and other facilities to the fragile Chad government. The UN have been left with few resources and told me they'd given up hope of getting helicopters for the mission.

As well as my work on the Council of Europe I've also taken a number of positions outside Parliament. Part of my rebuilding process has been to look at the kind of roles I might play when I leave. I was nervous dipping myself into the job market and have spent hours listening to head hunters and taking advice. As a result I am delighted to be on the boards of a number of bodies including Alcohol Concern, the British Healthcare Trade Association, the Council for Administration and Unlock – a great charity for ex-offenders run by a colourful ex-con, Bobby Cummines. I've also joined the board of a mental health charity as the issue is close to my heart.

Screwing Up

Of course the easiest way to earn money is via the celeb route. When you're involved in a scandal all sorts of calls come in. It's ironic that the very media that created your downfall suddenly become the source of employment and income. The most lucrative offer was from *I'm a Celebrity ... Get Me Out of Here!*. I'd always been a big fan of the programme so was rather amused when Belinda was asked to meet them in 2006. Nothing came of that and then a year later they made contact with me. Out of curiosity I went along to see the production team at ITV's studios on the South Bank. Against all my expectations I really liked the crew and suddenly found myself getting rather interested. Likewise I think they were surprised at how things went and before long we found ourselves in negotiations on a contract. Nobody I knew thought it was a good idea. 'Car crash TV' was the opinion of everybody I consulted about the pros and cons. But greed, ego and the whole idea of being in a remote jungle made me agree to appear. I wobbled a few times and they even got me to speak to Carol Thatcher about what it's really like. In the end I just lost my nerve and backed out an hour before signing the contract. I really messed them around and regret not having the balls to go through with it. I remember last November watching the ten o'clock news clips of Prime Minister's Questions with MPs shouting and screaming at each other and then flicking to ITV to see a bunch of celebrities chatting over a camp fire. The latter felt more dignified in many ways! At the end of the day it's just fun and you get to raise some cash for charity and, hopefully, make some new friends. I can see that now but at the time I guess I was still too raw from the whole tabloid experience to face the inevitable nasty comments.

Other offers have come and gone. In most cases I've refused although some have been irresistible. I jumped at the chance to do a celebrity quiz about *The West Wing*. I absolutely love that programme and when Channel 4 asked if I would team up with fellow fan Rory Bremner and David Tennant I could hardly contain my excitement. During some of the toughest periods around Westminster I used to collapse back at the flat with my box set of *The West Wing* wishing life round Whitehall was as inspiring as the White House.

Belinda and I have been protective of our home life but when *Celebrity Wife Swap* made contact I must confess I was again dazzled by the money on offer. Belinda, forever putting family first, vetoed the idea when we met up with the programme team. The only real regret I had about not doing *Celebrity Wife Swap* was the chance to exchange lives with someone else. I thought this would be a great social experiment, so when Channel 4 asked if I'd like to be included in a project that involved living on a council estate I jumped at the chance. It turned out to be one of the toughest weeks of my life, but with some amazing experiences.

There were various offers to do a kiss-and-tell book within months of my scandal. I spoke to a number of agents and decided that I did want to write a book, but I wanted it to be a serious political review of coalition governments. It hardly set the world alight. One agent put it bluntly: 'Well, you can do that and have your first book pulped, or you can have a bestseller on your private life.'

I was well aware of the choice but felt that part of my recovery process was to do something serious, not silly. I set about my book on coalitions with enormous enthusiasm and enjoyed researching the historical chapters on Gladstone, Ramsay MacDonald and the Great War coalitions. Equally, interviewing living politicians about more recent coalitions was a challenge as I sat with a Dictaphone and my own version of shorthand. The book was published in 2007 and I found the whole process incredibly therapeutic. I've not made a fortune but am glad I went down this route first before attempting this book. Of course writing this book has not been easy. I've had to tackle uncomfortable subjects but it's been a chance to take stock.

One of the bigger questions I face is about my future career. Once you say you're quitting you're endlessly asked what job you'll do next. It drives me mad and I am still not completely sure what I want to do. I've been for interviews in New York for international work and love the thought of a couple of years in Manhattan. I'd love to work for a charity as it would be a chance to focus on one issue in depth and I sense I'd make more of a difference to people's lives than I can in Westminster. Perhaps I'll have what is called a portfolio career, working on a few boards and doing media consultancy work.

A more radical idea is to set something up with Belinda and run a restaurant, shop or small business. She and her sister Julia are incredibly creative and it would be good to capture that in some way. A few years ago Belinda set up a little business called Clever Clogs, a range of easy-to-wear designer clogs for kids. It went really well as the children enjoyed shoes that fitted easily without the fiddle of laces and the Hampshire housewives got into the whole idea. Belinda managed to source a Polish supplier just outside Gdansk so we hired a car from Berlin and eight hours later in freezing conditions met up with these guys in a former abattoir to negotiate price and design. By the end of the meeting I was high on the smell of glue and the swigs of vodka we took to celebrate each stage of our agreement. God knows how, but a month later crates of clogs arrived on our doorstep and every shed and spare room was full of giraffe- and zebra-patterned clogs. The whole experience was exciting and rewarding but enormously hard work for little financial gain. It also showed me how small businesses can be killed off with tax, customs, VAT, health and safety forms and red tape. We don't make it easy for would-be entrepreneurs in this country.

One way or another I've been an elected politician for more than twenty years. As that period draws to a close I inevitably reflect on the past and try to predict a future. If I last as long as my dad then I am half-way through my life. Is the best over and the worst yet to come? It's a scary thought looking ahead but I know that politics has lost me money, friends and almost my family. Of course the failings have been mine but the demands of political life resulted in a drop in salary when I was elected as an MP, a drop in social life due to the hours and a devastating impact on our home life as I arrogantly chased political ambition when I should have been with Belinda and my two girls. That's a harsh judgement but on the positive side I've had experiences, good and bad, that will stay with me for life.

I've been flown over deserts by a Crown Prince in Dubai and Spanish soldiers in Chad. I've seen the horrors of slums in Kenya and war in Gaza. I've eaten rat in Burkina Faso and chased mice on the floor of the House of Commons. I've suffered grillings from Humphrys and Paxman and negotiated with Mr Bean and Mr Blair. My efforts have resulted in new laws for adopting children from overseas and helped hundreds of former prisoners of war held in Japan get compensation. I've been humiliated in the press, chased by paparazzi and become a hate figure on hundreds of blogs. I've run for party leader, won a by-election and been thrown out of Parliament by the courts. For thirteen years every Friday I have cried with constituents who are seriously ill, visited hospitals and schools, opened hundreds of fetes, dressed up as a penguin and Morris danced. I interrupted bath time, lovers and *EastEnders* as I knocked on about 50,000 doors over the years. Lying, crying and laughing became survival techniques to get through the weeks. I lied endlessly to conceal the truth over Charles Kennedy's drinking, I cried at refugee camps in Africa when children begged for attention and I laughed at my hopeless attempts on *University Challenge*.

All of this, however, will be forgotten. As a result of my own failings my name will be associated with scandal until the day I die. I am not proud of that but I am proud that I've survived that period of my life and feel stronger and happier as a result. If the future means more months at Vicarage Road, more laughing with friends, playing tennis and enjoying family time, well, then I am ready for those magic initials to disappear. Goodbye MP.

Index